CW00536151

The THEOLOGY *of the* BOOK *of* ISAIAH

John Goldingay

An imprint of InterVarsity Press
Downers Grove, Illinois

InterVarsity Press
P.O. Box 1400, Downers Grove, IL 60515-1426
World Wide Web: www.ivpress.com
Email: email@ivpress.com

InterVarsity Press® is the book-publishing division of InterVarsity Christian Fellowship/USA®, a movement of students and faculty active on campus at hundreds of universities, colleges and schools of nursing in the United States of America, and a member movement of the International Fellowship of Evangelical Students. For information about local and regional activities, write Public Relations Dept., InterVarsity Christian Fellowship/USA, 6400 Schroeder Rd., P.O. Box 7895, Madison, WI 53707-7895, or visit the IVCF website at www.intervarsity.org.

Cover design: Cindy Kiple
Interior design: Beth Hagenberg
Image: Turkish carpet ©semakokal/iStockphoto

ISBN 978-0-8308-4039-7 (print)
ISBN 978-0-8308-9619-6 (digital)

Printed in the United States of America ∞

InterVarsity Press is committed to protecting the environment and to the responsible use of natural resources. As a member of Green Press Initiative we use recycled paper whenever possible. To learn more about the Green Press Initiative, visit www.greenpressinitiative.org.

Library of Congress Cataloging-in-Publication Data
A catalog record for this book is available from the Library of Congress.

P 22 21 20 19 18 17 16 15 14 13 12 11 10 9 8 7 6 5 4 3 2 1
Y 34 33 32 31 30 29 28 27 26 25 24 22 21 20 19 18 17 16 15 14

Contents

Acknowledgments

Translations of the biblical text in this book are my own. The rationale for them and for my exegetical assumptions appears in the following places:

John Goldingay, *Isaiah* (Peabody, MA: Hendrickson; Carlisle: Paternoster, 2001).

———, *A Critical and Exegetical Commentary on Isaiah 56–66* (London/New York: Clark, 2013).

———, *The Message of Isaiah 40–55* (London/New York: Clark, 2005).

——— and David Payne, *A Critical and Exegetical Commentary on Isaiah 40–55* (London/New York: Clark, 2006).

Part two is an expansion of a chapter on "The Theology of Isaiah" in *Interpreting Isaiah*, ed. David G. Firth and H. G. M. Williamson (Leicester, UK: Inter-Varsity Press; Downers Grove, IL: IVP Academic, 2009).

Where I give a biblical reference in the form "64:12 [11]," the first verse number applies to English Bibles, the second to printed Hebrew Bibles.

I am grateful to Tom Bennett for reading the proofs and drawing up the subject index.

Introduction

My aim in this book is, first, to articulate the theology *in* the book called Isaiah—that is, to consider the theology expressed or implied by the different sections of Isaiah. I then aim to articulate the theology *of* the book called Isaiah as a whole, the theology that can be constructed *from* the book when one stands back and considers the whole.

When readers first open Isaiah, they may do so with two assumptions that make the book puzzling. One assumption is that the book will unfold in a clearly logical and coherent way, like a sermon with an introduction, three points and a conclusion. The other is that the entire book was written by Isaiah ben Amoz, the prophet whose name comes in the first line. Reading the book indeed puts a question mark by both assumptions.

Martin Luther once commented that the Prophets "have a queer way of talking, like people who, instead of proceeding in an orderly manner, ramble off from one thing to the next, so that you cannot make head or tail of them."[1] A book like Isaiah conveys that impression because it wasn't conceived by an author in the manner of this book that I'm writing, where I make a plan and know where I am going, and where (for the most part) I am writing from scratch and am beginning from the beginning, and where none of it exists until I write it. Isaiah is a collection of many prophecies

[1]Quoted from Gerhard von Rad, *Old Testament Theology* (New York: Harper & Row, 1962), 2:33. Luther was referring to the unsystematic way in which the Prophets mix up statements about contemporary Israel and about Christ (see *Lectures on the Minor Prophets II,* Luther's Works 19 [St. Louis: Concordia, 1974], p. 152).

that started off life as separate messages that were delivered on different occasions, and have subsequently been collected in this "book." In chapter 8, Isaiah tells us about an occasion when he himself collected some of his prophecies; Jeremiah 36 gives a more detailed account of when Jeremiah did the same thing.

Typically, a single "chapter" in Isaiah may include two or three or four prophecies that were delivered on different occasions (Isaiah 1 is a good opening example). Prophets, after all, were not essentially, necessarily or primarily writers. They were more like preachers. But they didn't deliver fifteen-minute sermons. To judge from the books that collect their prophecies, they delivered short messages that took two or three minutes to proclaim. They didn't have a captive audience, like a preacher; they stood and harangued people in the temple courts. They could perhaps assume that (like modern Westerners) people had short attention spans, or that people would soon move on from listening to one prophet to listening to another, or that they needed to say what they had to say before they got arrested.

So Isaiah is a kind of collage constructed from messages delivered in this way on different occasions. The implication is not that its organization is random; a collage may be purposefully put together. There will then be something to learn from its individual elements and also something to learn from the total arrangement. So it is with Isaiah. But we have to take a different approach to reading from the one we would take to a book such as Genesis or Ruth.

Actually I think of it as a collection of five or six collages, as follows:

Isaiah 1–12: messages and stories about Judah's life, about the trouble that threatens it and about the fulfillment of Yahweh's purpose for it. The concrete historical references relate to the time of King Ahaz (who reigned about 735–715), the first major stage of Isaiah's ministry.

Isaiah 13–27: messages about the nations around Judah, such as Babylon, Assyria, Philistia and Moab—both the big imperial powers and Judah's neighbors. Although these messages are about other nations, they are given as teaching to Judah. These individual peoples are in focus in chapters 13–23. Isaiah 24–27 then speaks about the world as a whole more than about individual nations.

Isaiah 28–39: more messages and stories about Judah's life, about the trouble that threatens it and about the fulfillment of Yahweh's purpose for it. It thus resembles chapters 1–12. But the concrete historical references now relate to the time of King Hezekiah (who reigned about 715–687), the second major stage of Isaiah's ministry.

Isaiah 40–55: messages to people living in the period when many Judahites had been transported to Babylon after the fall of Jerusalem in 587. More specifically, they are living on the eve of the moment when Cyrus, the Persian king, will conquer Babylon and free them to return to Judah, which happened in 539.

Isaiah 56–66: messages to the people in Judah itself sometime after 539, when they are rebuilding the temple or have rebuilt it but when the city is still in a devastated state.

Figure 0.1

One recurring feature in the collages is a description of God as "Israel's Holy One." So one can see the book as a whole as an outworking of this description of God, and see the collages in two sequences issuing from that fact about God:

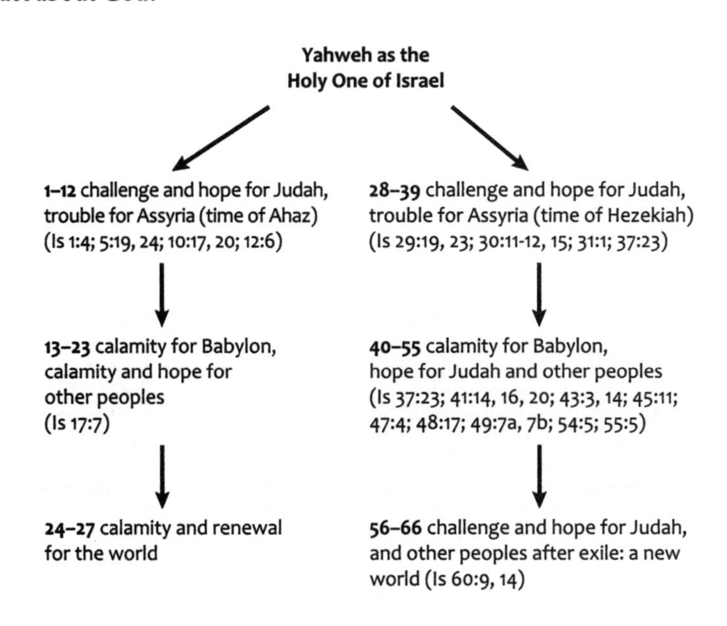

Figure 0.2

The different sections illustrate two ways of assembling a collage, which come out most clearly in the last two examples. Isaiah 40–55 is the section you can read most straightforwardly, in the sense that it works in quite a linear fashion. It's almost like a story or a logical argument; it works in ABCDEFG order. If you read (say) Isaiah 53 before Isaiah 42, you won't entirely get the significance of that later chapter. In contrast, Isaiah 56–66 works in a circular fashion—ABCDCBA. In other words, it will raise a subject then move onto another and another, and then work its way back through to where you started. There are several terms for this kind of collage—you can call it a ring composition, or a pyramid structure, or a stepped structure (you go up the steps then back down). But in Old Testament study the most common term is *chiasm*, so that's the one I will use.

Now the outline of the five collages points to something puzzling, which a Jewish commentator on Isaiah named Abraham Ibn Ezra had noticed in the twelfth century, four centuries before Luther.[2] This feature is the one that puts the question mark by that second assumption from which we began, the assumption that all the material in the book comes from Isaiah ben Amoz. Through Isaiah 1–39, the prophecies can be understood as speaking to people in Isaiah's day, the eighth century before Christ. When you get to Isaiah 40, things change. That chapter begins,

> Comfort, comfort my people, says your God.
> Speak to Jerusalem's heart, proclaim to it,
> That its tour of duty is fulfilled, that its waywardness is paid for,
> That it has received from Yahweh's hand double for all its offenses.

There is no dispute over the fact that the prophecy is addressing people who live a century and a half after Isaiah's day. Ibn Ezra thus inferred that Isaiah himself could hardly be the speaker.

Isaiah himself does speak about the future. He envisages Yahweh acting to punish Judah, looks beyond that event to Yahweh's restoring Judah, and speaks of a day when Yahweh will grant Judah a "new David," the person

---

[2]For the work of Ibn Ezra, see *The Commentary of Ibn Ezra on Isaiah*, trans. M. Friedländer (repr.; New York: Feldheim, 1964).

who will later be termed the Messiah. But in doing so, he speaks about what Yahweh *will do.* These events will happen in the future. In Isaiah 40–55 the difference is that the prophecy speaks in terms of what Yahweh *is doing* in the present. Now it is possible to imagine Yahweh transporting Isaiah into the distant future so that he speaks as if he is living then, and Yahweh certainly could do so, but it looks an odd thing for Yahweh to do. Ibn Ezra inferred rather that the prophecies beginning at Isaiah 40 come from a different prophet who lived among the people to whom he speaks, in that time 150 years after Isaiah ben Amoz. In some ways he does speak like Isaiah, and he shares Isaiah's views, and he shows that he knows Isaiah's prophecies. So we might call him a "Second Isaiah."

Four centuries after Luther, at the end of the nineteenth century, another German commentator, Bernhard Duhm, likewise suggested in an argument similar to Ibn Ezra's that another transition comes at Isaiah 56.[3] We have already noted that from then on, the prophecies look as if they address people who are back in Judah after the exile. They come, then, from a "Third Isaiah." Reading Isaiah 40–55 and 56–66 establishes that they have links with Isaiah 1–39 (and with each other), so it seems that the anonymous prophets whose work appears in these later parts of the book were in part inspired by Isaiah's prophecies, and that they saw themselves as furthering Isaiah's work and gaining part of their authority from their link with his. Such might be the reasons why they were content to have their prophecies appear in the same scroll as his.

There's no firm reason to assume that "Second Isaiah" was a single person who produced all of chapters 40–55 (though I myself think it likely) or that "Third Isaiah" was a single person who produced all of chapters 56–66 (I'm less sure about that question). Maybe there were a number of prophets whom Yahweh inspired to further Isaiah's ministry in this way. Further, it's plausible that people such as the hypothetical Second Isaiah had a hand in the development of Isaiah 1–39 and that the hypothetical Third Isaiah had a hand in the development of the book as a whole. But these possibilities

[3]For the work of Bernard Duhm, see *Das Buch Jesaia,* rev. ed. (Göttingen: Vandenhoeck, 1902).

will inevitably remain hypothetical. What we have in "the book called Isaiah" (H. G. M. Williamson's neat phrase)[4] is the collages. We will begin this study by looking at their individual messages or theologies, then look at the theology that emerges from the whole book. So when I refer to "the prophet" or "the prophecy" I do not imply any particular view about the prophet's identity, and in different contexts "Isaiah" may refer to the individual prophet Isaiah ben Amoz or to the book called Isaiah.

[4]The phrase comes from the title of H. G. M. Williamson's *The Book Called Isaiah* (New York: Oxford University Press, 1994). This book and Jacob Stromberg's *Isaiah After Exile* (New York: Oxford University Press, 2011) are examples of works that seek to trace the process whereby the book called Isaiah came into existence; see also Stromberg's *An Introduction to the Study of Isaiah* (New York: Clark, 2011).

PART ONE

The THEOLOGIES *in* ISAIAH

1

Isaiah 1–12

Old-fashioned movies and novels start at the beginning of a story and go through it in the order in which the events happened until they get to the end. More new-fangled movies and novels play games with their audiences and readers. They start in the middle, then flash back, then move forward again. They thereby make their audiences think harder. People don't get it unless they focus, and unless they let themselves become involved in the story.

Isaiah 1–12 is not a story in the strict sense, but it works a little like that new-fangled kind of story. Whereas Isaiah 40–55 has a linear arrangement and Isaiah 56–66 is a chiasm, Isaiah 1–12 has features of both these structures (which is one reason why it's complicated, in the way Luther noted in connection with the Prophets). And something of its theology is conveyed by that combination. On the one hand, the chapters affirm that Yahweh is intent on fulfilling a purpose with Judah and that its story is destined to go somewhere. On the other hand, in practice it's hard to see any progress in the story; what goes around comes around.

Faithfulness in the Exercise of Power

The opening chapters (Is 1:1–5:30) illustrate this point as they alternate between three themes. Precisely because each small section started off life as a separate message, the themes overlap between the sections, but they can be roughly distinguished as follows:

1. Judah is living as if it can ignore Yahweh's demands on its life (Is 1:2-20; 5:1-24)
2. Yahweh will therefore take action against it (Is 1:21-24, 28-31; 2:6–4:1; 5:25-30)
3. But Yahweh will restore it and turn it into what it should be (Is 1:25-27; 2:1-5; 4:2-6)

Implicitly, and occasionally explicitly, Isaiah indicates that Judah therefore needs to change its ways (e.g., Is 1:18-20) in order to short-circuit this sequence and make it possible for Yahweh to proceed to (3) without going via (2). But by the time the collage is put together, Judah had failed to change its ways, and (2) had happened. In this circumstance, (3) is the promise for the community to live by, but it will not come about unless Judah now hears the message expressed in (1) and reworks its life.

The problem is expressed most pungently in the "song" in Isaiah 5:1-7. Isaiah starts off like a singer entertaining people with a love song, which he says he has composed on behalf of a friend. It's a song about a vineyard, an image that love poetry often uses. But the love song veers off in a direction that's unexpected and then shocking. The vineyard produces no fruit; in other words, the man's courting gets him nowhere. He then turns from love to hate and destroys the vineyard. One might imagine other men listening to the singer-poet, sympathizing with him and with his action.

But the imagery of a vine was also familiar in another connection, and people listening to a prophet might have guessed that there was more to his song than met the eye. They would be familiar with the vineyard as an image for Israel, Yahweh being the vinedresser. Isaiah explains that his allegorical poem indeed refers to Yahweh and Israel. Yahweh too had looked for fruit and found only something that tasted nasty.

> He looked for *mišpāṭ*, but there—*miśpāḥ;*
> for *ṣĕdāqâ*, but there—*ṣĕʿāqâ*.

The conventional English translation of *mišpāṭ* and *ṣĕdāqâ* is "justice and righteousness," so that we might say that when Yahweh looked for *mišpāṭ* and *ṣĕdāqâ,* he was looking for social justice, but what Isaiah would mean by "social justice" has different connotations from those of the English expression. Here's a typical definition of social justice, by Innosanto Nagara:

> "Social Justice Work" is work that we do in the interest of securing human rights, an equitable distribution of resources, a healthy planet, democracy, and a space for the human spirit to thrive (read: arts/culture/entertainment). We do the work to achieve these goals on both a local and a global scale.[1]

These are commitments that Isaiah would sympathize with, but they don't correspond to *mišpāṭ* and *ṣĕdāqâ.*

Neither word has an English equivalent, as is the case with many Hebrew words related to theology and ethics. The broad meaning of *mišpāṭ* refers to government, the exercise of authority and the making of decisions. The King James Bible often translated it "judgment," and a positive aspect to this translation is that we expect judgment to be exercised in a way that is just (as we do with government, the exercise of authority and the making of decisions), but we know that it can be exercised in an unjust way. Similarly there can be perverted exercise of *mišpāṭ.* But "judgment" easily suggests a link with the proceedings of a court; furthermore, "judging" commonly has negative connotations. *Mišpāṭ* has positive connotations, and the exercise of power to which it refers is by no means confined to the making of decisions by a court.

The fact that *mišpāṭ* can be exercised in an unjust way links to its pairing with *ṣĕdāqâ.* Again, the common translation "righteousness" captures an aspect of *ṣĕdāqâ,* though "righteousness" is inclined to denote individual holiness, whereas *ṣĕdāqâ* is an essentially relational word. It suggests doing the right thing in relation to other people—in relation to God and to one's community. "Right" is thus nearer its connotations, but "faithful" is nearer still.

Mišpāṭ and *ṣĕdāqâ* thus suggests the faithful exercise of power in the community. People with power control resources; they will therefore make

---

[1]Quoted in Donna M. Riley, *Engineering and Social Justice* (San Rafael, CA: Morgan and Claypool, 2008), p. 4.

sure that ordinary people can share in resources such as land and food. People with power do control decision making in the court, which meets at the city gate; they will see that judicial decisions are made in a fair way. People with power control what happens in community worship; they will make sure that it is offered in a way that is faithful to Yahweh.

The problem is that Yahweh looks for *mišpāṭ* but sees *miśpāḥ;* he looks for *ṣĕdāqâ* but sees *ṣĕʿāqâ.* The word *miśpāḥ* comes only here in the Old Testament, though its connections with other words make its meaning clear enough. It denotes flowing—here, the flowing of blood that is involved in the oppression that is officially sponsored or tolerated in the community. Isaiah perhaps invented this word in order to pair it with *mišpāṭ.* It suggests the opposite to the proper exercise of *mišpāṭ.* Similarly *ṣĕʿāqâ* suggests the opposite to *ṣĕdāqâ,* in that it denotes an outcry or a cry of indignation or a cry of pain, the cry of the people who are being treated unfairly and oppressively. With horrific irony, it is a word used to describe Israel's crying out in Egypt, to which Yahweh responded in delivering people from their positions as state serfs there. It is now a cry that Israelites utter against one another.

The crop that Yahweh reaps in his carefully tended vineyard is one that makes him simply wish to abandon it to the elements.

HOLINESS

The center of the collage (Is 6:1–9:7 [6]) provides a further entry into understanding the dynamic of those opening chapters, by reviewing how Isaiah was involved in addressing people about the process those chapters implied. It begins with Isaiah's account of how he was commissioned to his confrontational ministry. He saw Yahweh exalted as king. It makes sense to picture Isaiah in the courtyards of the temple in Jerusalem, where in the sanctuary Yahweh was invisibly enthroned above the cherubim. It is the year the human King Uzziah died, an important year of transition as one king's reign gives way to another. Isaiah sees the invisible Yahweh (as it were), his robes filling the temple. The Hebrew word for "temple" is also the word for a king's palace, and the temple in Jerusalem was an earthly representation of Yahweh's heavenly palace. In Isaiah's vision, this earthly palace becomes the heavenly palace where Yahweh is enthroned as the real king of the universe. Isaiah's response is to realize that his lips are polluted; the reference to lips may relate to his being commissioned to use them as a prophet. He also refers to his people's lips being polluted, which must have a different point. His prophecies make clear that their lips are indeed polluted; their worship and social life are characterized by falsehood. After Isaiah's lips are purified, it becomes explicit that (like a human king) Yahweh is surrounded by his cabinet. This cabinet needs someone to undertake a task, and Isaiah volunteers to do so.

Christian reading of the chapter commonly stops when Isaiah says "Here am I—send me," but this reading thus confines itself to the preliminaries of the story. The commission is to tell Judah to listen and listen without understanding, and thereby to make it harder for people to see the reality of their situation and turn to Yahweh. That process will issue in devastation, comparable to the cutting down of a tree. It is no casual analogy, because Israel as the people of God is often likened to a tree.

At this point we have to recall that Isaiah's account of his commission is designed for Judah itself to hear. An irony is involved. The prophets' messages are commonly designed to be self-defeating, at a surface level, to shock people into the change that will mean Yahweh doesn't need to implement them. Their *underlying* aim is thereby achieved. Unfortunately, the strategy rarely works. (Jesus quotes these verses in Mark 4 in connection with his using the same technique; he also finds that it doesn't work.)

The last line of the chapter presupposes the failure of the shock tactic. The story thus needs to be read at two levels. It reflects the nature of Isaiah's actual ministry (when the possibility of Judah turning is still open), but it also reflects the later context in which this collage is being assembled (when it is known that Judah has not turned). The tree has been cut down. But the closing line (Is 6:13) adds the comment, "Its stump is the holy seed." There is the possibility that the tree can grow again.

The book's opening critique of the people was expressed in terms of their being people who have infuriated "Israel's Holy One" (Is 1:4). Just before the account of the commission, Isaiah has spoken of the scorn for "Israel's Holy One" that people's attitude implies (Is 5:19, 24). We have noted that this distinctive title for Yahweh recurs elsewhere in the book, and the word *holy* plays a key role in the story of Isaiah's commission. As well as being a vision of Yahweh as king, Isaiah's vision emphasizes that Yahweh is the "holy, holy, holy" one. The fact that Yahweh is king points toward the connotations of holiness. It suggests God's distinctively supernatural, dangerous, almost frightening, divine nature, which should make people bow their head simply because they are creatures—let alone because they are people polluted by their wrongdoing.

The point is further underlined by the association of the phrase "Yahweh Armies" with the phrase "Israel's Holy One." English translations usually have "LORD of Hosts" for the first of these two descriptions. They thus follow the usual practice of replacing the name Yahweh with the noun "LORD" (elsewhere in Isaiah 6, the word "Lord" printed thus does represent the regular Hebrew word meaning "Lord"). The word for "hosts" is the regular Hebrew word for armies, the word that appears on the back of Israeli military trucks. The expression looks as if it literally reads "Yahweh of Armies," which is an odd expression in Hebrew as in English, but one way or another it denotes the fact that Yahweh possesses or embodies all dynamic and forceful power, earthly and heavenly.

The holy God can associate earthly entities with him, and they then become holy, and also become dangerous. It's unwise to mess with them because God has identified with them. So Yahweh made Israel his holy people. That fact introduces danger into their own trivializing or compromising of their holy status, but it also adds to the rationale for Yahweh's not simply giving up on them (see Is 4:3 as well as Is 6:13). They are the holy seed.

TRUST

Isaiah's account of his commission leads into a story about his confronting the earthly king (Is 7). Judah is under pressure from Ephraim and Syria, and King Ahaz is out inspecting Jerusalem's defenses. The pressure from Ephraim and Syria links with the broader international context of pressure from Assyria, which wants to extend its empire westwards. Syria, then Ephraim, then Judah, are in its gun-sights.[2]

Isaiah takes with him a son named "Leftovers-will-return." The idea of leftovers is important in Isaiah, and there are several ways in which people could understand it. Yahweh is capable of dealing with Judah's foes in so radical a way that only leftovers will survive to go home and tell the tale; such is the promise Isaiah goes on to give Ahaz. But the account of Isaiah's commission has also given a warning that Yahweh's action against Judah itself will mean that only leftovers will survive. Isaiah 10 will later speak of the challenge to such leftovers to return to Yahweh.

Isaiah urges Ahaz not to be afraid but rather to trust in Yahweh. He makes the point by means of a neat double use of the Hebrew verb *'āman,* which the New Revised Standard Version captures nicely: "If you do not stand firm in faith, you shall not stand at all" (Is 7:9). Trusting Yahweh is a key motif in Isaiah's message. It is a key to Judah's avoiding a devastating fate. Isaiah also sees it as the proper response to that declaration concerning what Yahweh can do to Judah's attackers. He addresses the king as "David's household," which gives a further clue concerning why Ahaz should trust Yahweh's promises rather than being fearful. Yahweh had made a commitment to David and his successors. Isaiah puts before Ahaz a demandingly impractical expectation: that Israel should live its life in the world on the basis of trust in Yahweh rather than on the regular principles that nations and communities accept.

Isaiah adds further support for trust in inviting Ahaz to ask for a sign from Yahweh. Accepting a sign will put Ahaz in a difficult position, and he appeals to the Old Testament disapproval elsewhere of people testing Yahweh. Yahweh gives him a sign anyway. There is a girl who is going to have a baby, and when he is born she will be able to call him "God-is-with-us," in light of the way Yahweh has fulfilled his promises. Isaiah reiterates

---

[2]*Ephraim* is Isaiah's term for the northern kingdom that split off from Judah two centuries previously. The northern kingdom can also be referred to as "Israel" because it comprised most of the clans that had once been "Israel," but this usage is confusing, so I will also refer to it as Ephraim. When I speak of "Israel," I shall be referring to the people of God as a whole.

the same point by a different sort of sign when he himself begets a son (perhaps it is the same child) whom he names "Plunder-hurries-loot-rushes" (Is 8:1-4). The name promises the total defeat of Syria and Ephraim.[3]

Ahaz's refusal to trust Yahweh means the deliverance will do Judah no long-term good. The name "Plunder-hurries-loot-rushes" is also double edged: in the absence of trust by Ahaz, Judah's possessions, not those of Syria and Ephraim, will become loot. Isaiah restates these alternatives in a metaphor. Jerusalem's defenses crucially included its defense of its water supply, which came via the stream issuing from the Gihon spring and flowing to the Pool of Siloam. Those relatively placid waters provide an image for Yahweh's provision for Judah. But Judah has chosen not to trust in this provision. It will therefore find itself drowning in a more overwhelming flood.

There is a link between trust in Yahweh and the holiness of Yahweh. While any people might describe its gods as holy ones, and Israel is also prepared to describe other supernatural beings as holy ones, Yahweh is the Holy One par excellence, and the term comes to denote Yahweh's unique, extraordinary, awe-inspiring holiness as the only one who really deserves the title "God." His unique power and deity combined with his commitment to Israel (he is "Israel's Holy One") mean he can and should be trusted. To turn in other directions is not merely the underestimating of a friend; it is an affront to his holiness. Israel can be in awe of all sorts of things (Assyria, Ephraim, Syria, alien gods). It needs to be in awe of Yahweh alone as the Holy One.

Darkness and Light

Isaiah determines simply to sit and wait for Yahweh to do what he has said (Is 8:17). Yahweh has told him to write down his teaching among his disciples—these might be Yahweh's disciples, or they might be Isaiah's disciples, though it makes little difference. Either way, they are people who have taken some notice of Isaiah. Writing down Yahweh's threats will give

---

[3]On the New Testament reference to Isaiah 7:14, see "A Note on Isaiah's Role in the New Testament" on pp. 32-36.

something for Isaiah to point to when they are implemented; writing down the promises of a restoration that could follow will give people something hopeful to consider at that point.

Instead of taking any notice of Isaiah, most people are inclined to consult mediums and other spiritual experts, who can put them in touch with relatives who have passed and who, because they are not confined to this life, may be able to give them advice about the suppliants' lives and future (Is 8:19-20). People who consult the dead need not see themselves as being disloyal to Yahweh: the dead are in Yahweh's care, and consulting them is a means of discovering what Yahweh has to say. But it's the traditional gods' way, not Yahweh's way, and operating in this fashion means that in effect they are consulting the traditional gods, not consulting Yahweh. They are resorting to darkness in order to find their way through dark times, but they will find themselves in even greater darkness, gloom and murkiness.

Surprisingly, at this point (Is 9:2-7 [1-6]) there comes a declaration that light has dawned. Darkness is a figure for a situation where one does not understand what is going on, for an experience of trouble, for deception and plotting, and for death itself (a tomb is a dark place). It thus suggests a realm from which Yahweh is absent or in which he is inactive. Light is a figure for a situation where one can see and understand, for a place where one doesn't mind being seen, for an experience of deliverance and blessing, for a realm where Yahweh is present and active.

In Isaiah's day Israel experienced both darkness and light. The collage here juxtaposes the community's experience of darkness and the prospect of deeper gloom, and also the experience of dawning light and the prospect of full brightness. Perhaps darkness is deepening and light is dawning at the same time, or perhaps the deepening and the dawning belong in different contexts. The collage holds both before its readers, to offer them challenge and hope.

Strikingly, the dawning of light takes the form of the deliverance of Ephraim. There was no such deliverance in Isaiah's day; Isaiah's description of a dawning that has happened is actually a description of a dawning that lies in the future. There are other passages in Isaiah and elsewhere where promises about the future are expressed as if the events have already happened; if Yahweh has decided to make it happen, it is already actual.

Isaiah goes on to speak of another child, one who has been born, who will rule with authority on David's throne with *mišpāṭ* and *ṣĕdāqâ*. Like earlier children who have been mentioned, he will have a name that will speak of Yahweh's activity: "An-extraordinary-planner-is-the-warrior-God; the-everlasting-Father-is-an-officer-for-well-being." Like those other names, this one does not describe the child but proclaims something that his birth is to remind people of, something about their God. Their warrior God is a great counselor, one capable of formulating plans and fulfilling them. And their everlasting Father is an officer or leader who will bring them *šālôm* or well-being.

The other births that have been reported are events that have already happened; so perhaps has this birth. The child will then be King Hezekiah, in whose time Yahweh did prove himself along lines suggested by the name, and in whose time light did dawn, though his reign was not the beginning of a new age. Yet the declaration about deliverance spoke in the past tense about something that had not yet taken place. It likely follows that this birth is also an event to come; Isaiah 11 is explicit that the emergence of such a king lies in the future.

Putting Down and Raising Up

In due course Isaiah turns his fire on the nation that will be the means of Yahweh's disciplining Israel, and elaborates further on Israel's restoration (Is 10:5–12:6).

In Isaiah, Yahweh uses human agents, particularly imperial powers, to express both his anger and his faithfulness toward Israel. Assyria, Babylon and Persia fulfill this role. Isaiah uses vigorous language to describe Yahweh's controlling direction of them. Yahweh had "whistled" for Assyria like a general whistling for his forces (or his dog?) (Is 5:26; 7:18). Here, Yahweh "sends" Assyria and "commissions it," as he had sent Isaiah (Is 6:8). Yet an army is aware of the general whistling, and a prophet is aware of Yahweh sending. Assyria is not only a conscript but an unconscious one. It undertakes action against Judah for its own reasons. It is aware of its power and skill, likes using them, and in particular likes using them so as to increase its own wealth.

Yahweh's attitude is that a superpower ought to recognize that it serves a higher power. A club sits in the hand of someone who wields it. Assyria behaves as if it is self-wielding; to be even more paradoxical, it behaves as if it wields the person who holds it, rather than the other way around. Like Amos in his condemnation of the nations surrounding Ephraim (and like Paul in Romans), Isaiah assumes that nations have an inbuilt knowledge of their relationship to God, their subordination to God and their responsibility to God, and an inbuilt knowledge of what counts as right ways of behavior. They don't need a special revelation concerning the basics of right and wrong. If they ignore that knowledge and simply do as they wish, they are responsible for their actions and may pay for them. Although it has unwittingly implemented Yahweh's will, Assyria will pay for the fact that its motivation lay in a different direction.

The impressive Assyrian tree is therefore to be felled and/or burned, sharing the fate of the not-so-impressive Judahite tree of whose felling and burning Isaiah has already spoken. But the prophecy has already indicated that the devastating of that tree will leave it with a tiny basis for new growth. That prospect reappears in Isaiah 11:1-10, where the image of a tree, its felling and its renewed growth is applied to the Davidic line, as well as to the people as a whole.

Isaiah 11 is the nearest to a "messianic" promise in this first collage. It does not use the word *māšîaḥ,* which never appears in the Old Testament with reference to a future king (in Isaiah, it comes only in Is 45:1, where it refers to Cyrus). But the passage does speak of a future king of the Davidic line who will fulfill Yahweh's vision for the Davidic king in a way that Ahaz doesn't, and that even Hezekiah will not. He will be an embodiment of insight, not stupidity, unlike both these kings, who lacked insight in the way they conducted national affairs. He will walk in Yahweh's way in ruling the people and will encourage the people as a whole in that direction. He will implement *mišpāṭ* and *ṣĕdāqâ* in the country and thus work on behalf of ordinary people rather than powerful people. He will take violent action against the powerful so that the powerless will thus no longer be at their mercy, like sheep that no longer have to fear wolves.

Within Isaiah's lifetime, Assyria conquers Ephraim and transports many of its people, and in due course a similar fate will overcome Judah. When the Judahite tree or the Assyrian tree is felled and burned, only "leftovers" will remain, and some of Judah's leftovers will find themselves scattered around the countries to the west, the south and the east. But Yahweh will reach out to fetch both Judahites and Ephraimites back, and will also transform relationships between Ephraim and Judah, and between both of them and their neighbors (Is 11:11-16).

Things Move Forward, but What Goes Around Comes Around

We have noted the way that the arrangement of individual prophecies in this collage gives it some forward movement but also some impression that what goes around comes around. At its center is the portrayal of Isaiah's activity and its implications in Isaiah 6:1–9:7 [6], which is set in the context of a series of solemn confrontations and proclamations of Yahweh's anger.

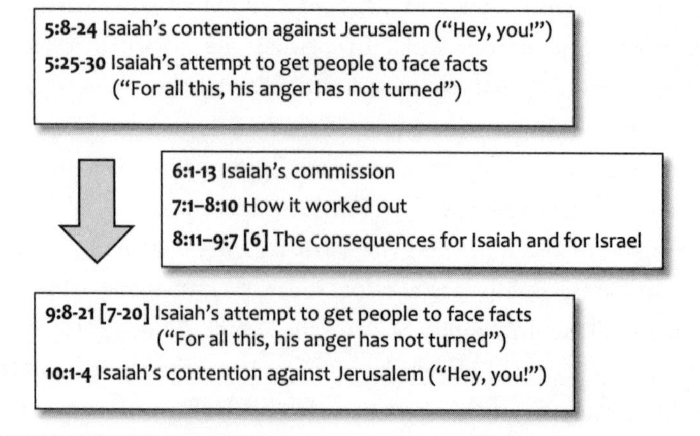

Figure 1.1

A tension between judgment and comfort already appeared in the opening sections of the collage (Is 1:1–5:7), and it reappears in the closing ones (Is 10:5–12:6). In the opening part, Isaiah paints long descriptions of Israel, Judah and especially Jerusalem, and of the disaster that must come, but alternates these with lyrical pictures of how things will be when Jerusalem is restored. If the more somber picture dominates the opening, the closing part becomes increasingly encouraging. After the last contention against Jerusalem, Isaiah turns to speak the same "Hey, you!" to the one who is to be the means of Jerusalem's punishment; more pictures of Yahweh's restoration of Israel follow. The collage then closes with a song to sing in the day Yahweh fulfills these promises.

So chapters 1–12 as a whole unfold as follows:

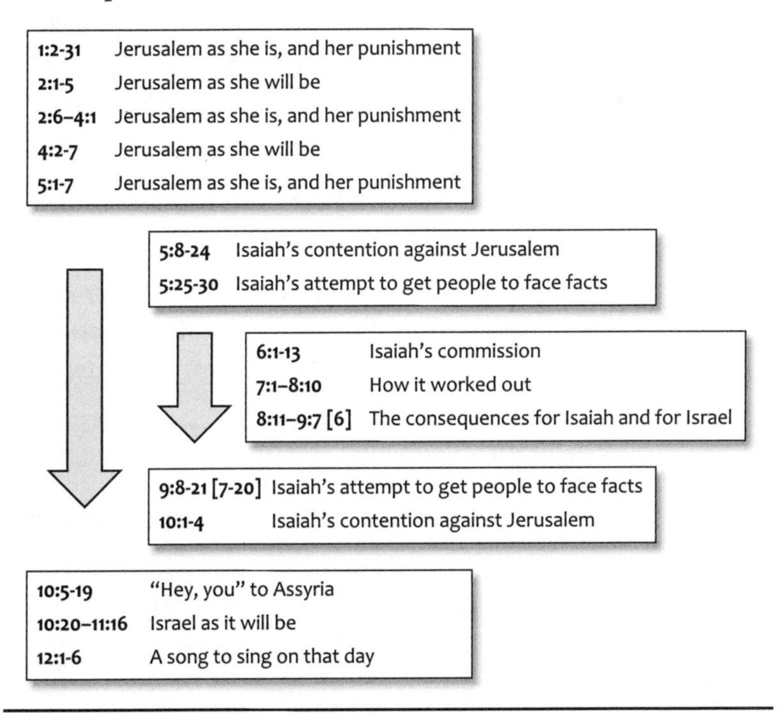

Figure 1.2

The theological implication of the collage as a whole is to affirm both that things move forward and that what goes around comes around. Perhaps it would be better to reverse the order. What goes around comes around, but that alternation does not have the last word. Yahweh is committed to bringing the sequence to an end. Israel's experience is not condemned to being an eternal cycle. It constitutes a spiral. The song to sing "on that day," which closes off this first collage, makes that point. There will be a time when Israel can look back on the fulfillment of the promise of deliverance and enjoy ongoing blessings, when "great in your midst is Israel's Holy One" (Is 12:6).

A Note on Isaiah's Role in the New Testament

The New Testament begins with a compressed summary of the Old Testament story in the form of an account of Jesus' ancestry, and then goes on to a series of vignettes that make up the story of his birth and the initiation of his ministry, in which quotations from the Prophets play a prominent role. In the first of these vignettes, Matthew 1:18-25, his birth is recounted in light of Isaiah 7:14:

> Look, the virgin will have a child in the womb and will give birth to a son,
> and will call his name Emmanuel.

Jesus' ministry then happens against the background of the ministry of John the Baptizer. He is introduced in Matthew 3:1-3, where Matthew describes John as "the person spoken of through Isaiah the prophet when he said,

> The voice of someone shouting in the wilderness,
> "Prepare the Lord's way, straighten his paths." (Is 40:3)

In Matthew 4:14-17, the Gospel writer then links Jesus' beginning his own preaching in Galilee with Isaiah 9:1-2 [8:23–9:1]:

> Country of Zebulun and country of Napthtali,
> the way of the sea, beyond the Jordan, Galilee of the nations:
> the people sitting in darkness has seen a great light;
> for those sitting in a region and in deathly shadow—light has dawned for them.

In Matthew 8:14-17 Matthew goes on to link Jesus' healing ministry with Isaiah 53:4:

> He himself took our illnesses and carried away our diseases.

In Matthew 12:15-21 the Gospel writer interprets Jesus' desire that people not make a public issue of his healing ministry by quoting Isaiah 42:1-4:

> Look, my servant whom I chose, the one I love,
>   in whom I myself delighted:
> I shall put my spirit on him;
>   he will announce judgment to the nations.
> He will not argue or shout,
>   nor will anyone hear his voice in the streets.
> A bent reed he will not break,
>   a flickering wick he will not snuff out,
> until he brings judgment to victory,
>   and in his name nations will hope.

The pattern of quotation continues in Matthew; it also appears in the other Gospels and elsewhere in the New Testament. In Matthew and elsewhere there are also many allusions to Isaiah that are not identified as such (see, for instance, Jesus' blessings in Mt 5:3-12, and his account of his ministry in Mt 11:4-5). But the examples of actual quotation give us enough material to consider the questions they raise.

It is the rule rather than the exception that Matthew's quotations ignore the meaning of the passages in their context in Isaiah. While there is some uncertainty about whether Isaiah 7 is talking specifically about a girl who is a virgin at the moment, or whether she is a young married woman, if she is a virgin there is no suggestion in the context that she will still be a virgin when she has her baby; further, the context suggests a birth to take place in the near future, not in some centuries' time. Isaiah 40 is talking about God's intention to return to Jerusalem in the sixth century B.C. Isaiah 9 refers to the situation of Israel in Isaiah's day. Isaiah 53:4 does not refer to someone who will take away people's infirmities but to someone who has already shared their suffering. Isaiah 42 describes the servant as someone who does not make a noise about his own suffering.

How may one understand theologically the fact that Matthew uses the words in Isaiah in a way that ignores their meaning in their context?

The New Testament writers were people who had been grasped by Jesus and had recognized that God has sent him as the definitive means of putting into effect God's longstanding intentions for the world. They recognized, further, that things God had done and said that appear in the Scriptures would therefore surely cohere with and illumine what God did and said in Jesus. God was pursuing a goal in the story the Scriptures told and was indicating in the Scriptures intentions that related to that goal. It was to be expected that things Jesus did or that happened to him would constitute the achievement of that goal and the realization of those intentions.

The New Testament writers thus look back into the Scriptures for illustrations of these facts about Jesus. Their process of interpretation does not start from a reading of Isaiah that reveals God's intentions or expectations and moves toward Jesus, and it does not seek to establish that Jesus is the Messiah on the basis of such an argument. The process moves in the opposite direction, from Jesus back into the Scriptures. The New Testament writers know that Jesus is the Messiah and know that his execution was not an odd event but the key event for the fulfillment of God's purpose. They need to be able to come to understand what Jesus being the Messiah means and what his execution means. They thus look back into the Scriptures for help in answering those questions.

Modern scholarly Christian study of this question would be likely to approach it by asking what the texts in Isaiah did mean in their historical context and working forward from that understanding to an understanding of Jesus. The operation would be historical, logical, analytical and rational. Ordinary Christian study of Scripture is more intuitive and pays more attention to parallels in wording than to establishing what the words meant in their historical context. It thus parallels the New Testament use of the Scriptures, which itself parallels the approach to interpretation taken by other Jewish groups in New Testament times. These other Jewish groups did not accept the same starting point as the Jews who believed in Jesus, but they would have accepted their approach to discovering the meaning of the Scriptures by starting from current faith convictions and questions and looking at the Scriptures in light of them.

Isaiah's promise about a girl having a baby whose birth would signify that God was with his people in the crisis they were going through was not a promise about something to happen in seven centuries' time, nor was it a prophecy about a girl who would still be a virgin when she had her baby, nor about a baby who would turn out to be the very embodiment of God. No regular Jewish interpretation in Jesus' day would have understood the passage to refer to the Messiah. But when Jesus was born of someone who was actually still a virgin and when he turned out to be the very embodiment of God, Matthew's eyes popped when he noted that prophecy in Isaiah. It helped him put a label onto realities that the early Christians knew and to see them in the context of the scriptural story. Something similar is true about the other passages quoted above, and other passages in the New Testament that refer back to Isaiah.

In the interpretation of Scripture, one can make a useful distinction between meaning and significance. When God inspired prophetic Scripture, it had a God-given *meaning* for the prophet and for the people whom the prophet addressed, and the written version had a meaning for the writer and for the people who originally read the prophetic scroll. The presupposition of preserving the scroll is that it could have further *significance* for people who read it later. For instance, Matthew uses Isaiah 53:4 to illumine an understanding of Jesus' healing ministry. Christians have often assumed that Isaiah 52:13–53:12 literally refers to Jesus, but the New Testament also assumes that the *significance* of Isaiah 53 is not limited to this reference. The chapter has a *significance* for understanding the vocation of the church (see Phil 2:1-11; 1 Pet 2:19-25). A reference to the church is not part of the *meaning* of Isaiah 52:13–53:12; it is part of its *significance.* The same is true of a reference to Jesus.

There is a sense in which passages in Isaiah have more than one meaning. There can be a difference between the meaning of a prophecy when a prophet uttered it and its meaning in the context of his written scroll. For instance, Isaiah 42:1-4 in itself forms a description of the role of Yahweh's servant without identifying that servant. Yet in its place in the book, what has preceded in Isaiah 41 has identified the servant as Israel, what will follow later in Isaiah 42 will make explicit that Israel cannot fulfill this role, and subsequent chapters will take further the question of who does fulfill it. One might say that Isaiah 42:1-4 has a meaning in itself but also has further significance when seen in its context. As this process unfolds, early stages in discovering the prophecy's significance become part of its meaning. Once the book reaches its final form, its meaning freezes, but its significance is unlimited.

The implication of the New Testament's use of Isaiah is not that the text of Isaiah has a further meaning other than the one it had for the prophets whose words appear in the book and for the people to whom they spoke or for whom the book was written. It does not have a deeper meaning or a spiritual meaning or a fuller meaning; it just has a meaning. But it does have vast potential for further significance when read in different contexts.

In connection with Paul's adapting Isaiah 64:4 [3] to a point he wishes to make, John Calvin comments that Paul seems to "torture" the text "to a different purpose" from the one it has in its context: "in this respect the Apostles were not squeamish; for they paid more attention to the matter than to the words, and reckoned it enough to draw the attention of the reader to a passage of Scripture, from which might be obtained what they taught."[4] One could make a similar point about the way Paul takes up Isaiah 65:1-2 in Romans 10:20-21, where he applies 65:1a to the way God has become available to peoples other than Israel in his day, and 65:2a to the way God has reached out to Israel in vain in his day. The broader context in Isaiah 65:1–66:24 does match the point Paul makes. The *content* of the New Testament matches that of Isaiah, even if the *verbal links* that the New Testament makes ignore the *meaning* of particular words in Isaiah. The fact that God inspired the prophecy with its inherent meaning makes it worthwhile to seek to understand that meaning and not to confine ourselves to reading Isaiah through the spectacles provided by the *significance* that the New Testament sees in it.

[4]John Calvin, *Commentary on the Book of the Prophet Isaiah* (repr.; Grand Rapids: Eerdmans, 1956), 4:364.

2

Isaiah 13–27

The opening words of this second collage announce a change of focus, as they give as a title for the next section, "A prophecy about Babylon." While Isaiah 10 has spoken of the destiny of Assyria, the chapters that now follow speak of the destiny of a series of other peoples in Judah's world. The horizon thus broadens. At Isaiah 24:1 the horizon broadens again; four further chapters speak about the world as a whole. So Isaiah 1–27 keeps extending the horizon:

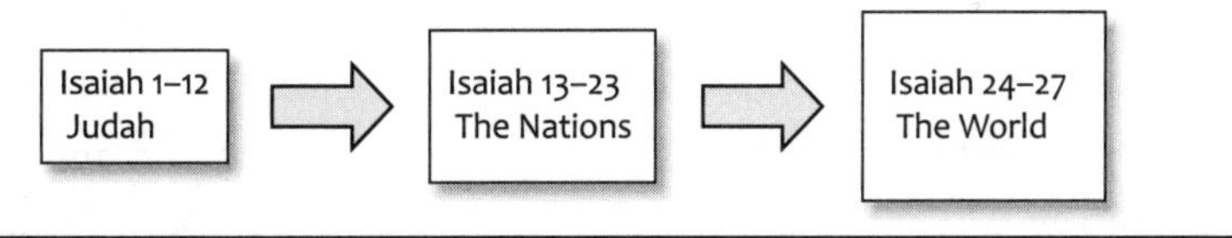

Figure 2.1

The Nations (Isaiah 13–23)

Chapters 13–23, then, deal with many of the peoples in Judah's world:

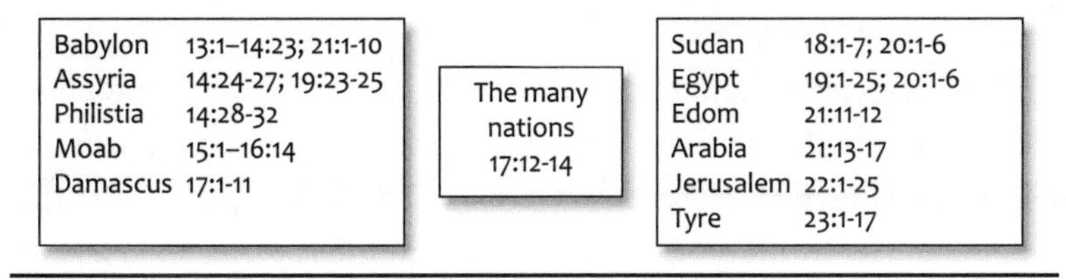

Figure 2.2

These chapters are often described as prophecies *against* the nations, and for the most part they do speak of trouble that is coming to other peoples, not of their blessing. Yet the text of Isaiah simply calls them by titles such as the "Babylon prophecy" and the "Moab prophecy." This more neutral description links with the fact that in most cases, as far as we know, they aren't delivered to the nations to which they refer. They are delivered to the Judahites, like the rest of the prophecies. They would be effective in implementing God's intentions for these nations, since they were the word of Yahweh that put Yahweh's purpose into effect, but their delivery is part of a prophet's ministry to the people of God. The Philistia prophecy might be an exception, since it's associated with the arrival of envoys from Philistia in Judah.

There are three reasons for telling Judah about them. Their focus on disaster links with Judah's understandable inclination to be afraid of many of these nations. Judah needs to be reminded that Yahweh is Lord in political events and to trust in Yahweh's capacity to put down attackers and oppressors. The obverse is that Judah is inclined to trust in some of these nations as its means of deliverance from political pressures. This inclination is another reason for Yahweh to affirm his lordship of these nations and his capacity to put them down. Judah is not to trust in them rather than trusting in Yahweh. The point is explicit in the prophecy about Egypt and Sudan (Egypt's dynasty at the time was Sudanese), where Isaiah goes about Jerusalem stripped and barefoot to represent the coming fate of these nations on whom other people were trusting and to whom they were fleeing for help and rescue (Is 20:6).

The questions of fear and trust relate to contexts where Judah is under threat. Isaiah also talks about peoples who are more or less irrelevant to Judah, in the enigmatic prophecies referring to Dumah, Dedan, Teman and Qedar (desert places away to the east; Is 21:11-17) and in the Tyre prophecy (Is 23:1-18). Prophecies such as these raise Judah's eyes from its own concerns and remind it that Yahweh is lord of all the nations, even ones that are nothing to do with Judah. These prophecies thus prepare the way for the visions concerning the whole world in Isaiah 24–27. For subsequent readers, they offer theological insight on the way God looks at nations in general and superpowers in particular.

The Day of Yahweh

Since before Isaiah's time, Israel had looked forward to a great day when its enemies would be punished and Israel would enter into God's fullest blessing. Amos 5:18-20 warns about such hopes. Isaiah, too, has already talked about the fact that "Yahweh Armies has a day against all majesty and exaltedness, against all that is high" (Is 2:12; see further Is 2:13-16). While a listener who drifted past as Isaiah was making this proclamation would assume he was declaring the downfall of a mighty nation such as Assyria, he has already made clear that actually he is speaking about Judah.

The prophecy about Babylon now speaks once more about Yahweh's day as a day of destruction, a day of Yahweh's angry blazing (Is 13:6-13). The significance of Yahweh's day has been reversed again, restoring to it something like the meaning it had in the popular thinking that Amos opposed. The superpower's downfall is Yahweh's day happening before people's eyes, the day when Yahweh puts down his people's adversaries, a day of military victory by Yahweh and his heavenly forces. This way of describing Yahweh's day links with the use of the title "Yahweh Armies," which comes frequently in the prophecies about the nations. It's an appropriate way to speak of God in connection with a day when the forces of heaven and earth are in battle.

There is a finality attached to the idea of Yahweh's day, yet not the kind of finality that means history comes to an end. There is an ultimacy about this day, yet it happens in history. Further, it is a day that can happen more than once. Testimony to this fact comes in Lamentations, a set of prayer-poems from after the fall of Jerusalem in 587. The day of the city's fall was "the day of his angry blazing" (Lam 1:12). "You yourself acted, you brought about the day you proclaimed" (Lam 1:21). Yahweh's day had arrived for Jerusalem. So this day is not the final judgment, but a moment when God's ultimate purpose receives one of its periodic partial fulfillments in history, as pride is put down and the oppressed are delivered. A pattern characteristic of prophecy appears here. It speaks as if the end of the world is imminent; what fulfills such prophecies is not the actual end, but a particular historical expression of God's ultimate purpose receiving a fulfillment in time.

The fall of Babylon will be such a moment. Prophecies about Babylon come first in Isaiah 13–23, which in the context of Isaiah's lifetime is odd; in his day, Babylon was not the great power, and it was a long way away from Judah. Isaiah 21:1-10 is another prophecy about Babylon in the midst of the prophecies about other peoples, and it represents more what one might have expected of a prophecy against Babylon in Isaiah's lifetime.

A promise in the midst of Isaiah 13–14 offers a clue to Babylon's prominence here. In the Hebrew text, the Babylon prophecy as a whole divides into two sections after what is numbered as Isaiah 14:1-2 in English Bibles; thus Isaiah 13:1-22 leads straight into 14:1-2. These two verses point to the reason for the Babylon prophecy's prominence, as they promise that Yahweh will again have compassion on Israel and settle Israel in its own country. Two centuries after Isaiah's day, Babylon will have taken over the position of superpower from Assyria and will have taken many Judahites into exile. It will then be Babylon that needs putting down if Yahweh is to have compassion on Judah. Delivering Israel and putting down its oppressors must go together. As Mary puts it, "scattering the proud" and "exalting the lowly" are two sides of a coin (Lk 1:51-52).

The link between the Babylon prophecy and the Judahites' exile might suggest that the Babylon prophecy comes not from Isaiah but from a prophet ministering two centuries later. But there are other possibilities. While Babylon was not yet a major power in Isaiah's day, it was an up-and-coming one; hence its appearance in the story in Isaiah 39. One would expect Isaiah to have talked about Babylon, and the arrangers of the collage might have given prominence to his message about Babylon because of Babylon's later importance. Yet the actual prophecies make little specific reference to Babylon, which is named only in the introductions to the prophecies (Is 13:1; 14:4) and then in Isaiah 13:19; 14:22. Further, Babylon's prominence in Isaiah 13–23 contrasts with the small amount of attention given to Assyria (see Is 14:24-27), even though Assyria is much more important in the time of Isaiah ben Amoz (Assyria has of course been covered in Isaiah 10). Possibly, then, the Babylon prophecies are a reworking of Isaiah's own prophecies about Assyria, reapplying them to Babylon. It reflects how the Old Testament can see the succession of superpowers (Assyria, Babylon, Persia, Greece) as embodiments of one phenomenon. The same implication emerges from Isaiah 33, which simply talks about "the destroyer" and "the betrayer." The Babylon prophecy thus suggests a theological insight about superpowers. It also suggests another about prophecies, which are open to reapplication in new contexts when the same dynamics recur. That reapplying happens even within Scripture.

The Archetypal Superpower

At the center of the prophecies about the nations, Isaiah 17:12-14 explicitly promises the fall of any superpower that arises, picturing the disappearance of "the nations" that rage and roar and plunder. Hebrew has no term that simply denotes "the superpower" or "the empire," and in such contexts "the nations" or "the peoples" are set over against nations and peoples such as Judah that are their victims and underlings.

In these dynamics there is also a link with the way Babylon became *the* symbol of a nation set over against God, as it is in the Revelation to John. The collage's arrangement may imply it is already becoming such a symbol. The Babylon whose fall is described is then not merely the historical Babylon, Israel's conqueror, but also the symbolic Babylon. Its fall signifies the dethroning of every power opposed to God.

There is a further feature of the superpowers' interrelationship. As the agent of Babylon's fall, Yahweh will arouse the Medes (Is 13:17). It is a different image from "whistling" for Assyria but a similar reality. Indeed, Yahweh also speaks of summoning them and shouting to them. Assyria, Babylon, Medo-Persia—without realizing it, each is Yahweh's agent; each gets put down by the next agent in line. In their capacity as his agents, Yahweh can describe the Medes as "people I have sanctified" (Is 13:3).

Isaiah 14 goes on to taunt Babylon's king, in a funeral dirge sung for a king who is at present very much alive (compare Amos's funeral dirge on Israel in Amos 5:2). The prophecy imagines Israel relieved of oppression and in a position to exult over God's judgment on wickedness, picturing the event as the fall of one who had tried to make himself into God. We should not attempt to identify a particular king; the point does not lie in the attitude of an individual. It is associated with being ruler of the superpower.

Isaiah utilizes motifs that his audience would recognize as coming from foreign myths. The prophecy addresses the Babylonian king as "Morning star, son of the dawn" (Is 14:12), taking up titles of Canaanite gods. Babylonian and Canaanite myths told of gods who tried to take over the power of the highest god; Isaiah uses such stories as parables of the Babylonian king's presuming to take God-like authority over the whole world. The literal morning star is Venus, which appears just before the sun each day but is then eclipsed by the sun. The Babylonian king will collapse as readily as Venus does each morning.

"Morning star" is also the expression translated "Lucifer" ("Light-bearer") in the King James Bible, and this passage in Isaiah came to be understood as an account of the fall of Satan. In the myths that Isaiah is using, it does have such a significance, but the Bible uses the story only as a parable about something happening on earth. Ezekiel 28:12-19 reapplies the same myth to the king of Tyre.

The prophecies focus on declaring that the nations are going to fall, because that fact is the point as far as Judah is concerned. They speak only briefly about the reasons why the nations must fall. The first reason is their majesty and their associated arrogance (Is 13:11, 19), which fits with the earlier critique of Assyria and of Judah itself (cf. also Is 16:6). When you have reason for pride (in your real importance and power), it's almost impossible not to fall into pride and therefore to need to be put down. The dynamic is the one associated with the king of Babylon (Is 14:12-15). A second reason is that, conversely, it is morally necessary for the lowly to be lifted up and the underlings exalted. Isaiah does not assume that everyone will therefore be equal. There will continue to be bosses and underlings, but people's positions will be reversed, as Jesus assumes when he speaks of disciples judging Israel's clans (Mt 19:28; Lk 22:30). Third, Yahweh also speaks of exposing the powerlessness of the nations' so-called gods and the uselessness of their so-called insight and capacity to decide what will happen in the world (e.g., Is 19:1-17).

In the Jerusalem prophecy, in light of the general significance of these prophecies for Judah, it is appropriate that the critique focuses on the city's concern for its military defenses and its neglect over looking to its maker, the shaper of its destiny (Is 22:11). In Tyre's case, while the disaster will deal with the arrogance that it shares with other great peoples (Is 23:11), the chapter focuses more distinctively on Tyre's position as a great trading nation. The Prophets are inclined to disapprove of trade as a means of making money—the exchange of surplus goods should be a mutual sharing of resources. Treating it as a way of increasing one's wealth turns trade into prostitution (Is 23:15-18).

There is a particular reason for the Babylonian king's fall: "you have destroyed your country and slaughtered your people" (Is 14:20). While a leader may argue that prestigious building projects and making war to extend the empire benefit his people, in the short term, at least, his people pay a price for the implementation of the leader's plans. They pay taxes, and they go off to risk their lives in battle. The king's death and the termination of his dynasty is therefore good news for his own people.

Hope for the Nations

There is a sense, then, in which the fall of the superpower is good news for the peoples of Babylon and of the empire as a whole. Most of the prophecies explicitly or implicitly incorporate some hope for the nations—for instance, by escaping judgment or finding mercy after judgment. Yahweh's stance toward them is thus not so different from his stance toward Judah. A related feature discouraging Judah from an unequivocally negative stance toward the nations is that one of the chapters concerns Jerusalem, hinting that Judah is no better than these foreign nations and that Yahweh's way of relating to the other nations will indeed also be his way of relating to Judah. There is no room for Judah's thinking that its position as the people of God means it will escape if its stance toward Yahweh is no different from theirs. Ephraim also appears, in association with Syria, in Isaiah 17:1-11.

The Babylon prophecy introduces the note of hope for the nations, in an ambiguous way (Is 14:1-2). Foreigners will "join" Jacob's household; the verb is the one later used of conversion. But "peoples" will also submit to Israel's authority as Israel once submitted to its captors. The verses present different destinies before a superpower. Even for Babylon, all is not lost. Its coming fall is described in horrific terms: the Medes will smash Babylon's babies before its eyes; this prophecy lies behind the prayer in Psalm 137, which is not dreaming up something horrific out of human imagination but simply asking Yahweh to do as he said. It is the kind of thing that happens in war. But in the event Babylon surrendered to the Persian army and did not experience the kind of atrocity of which Isaiah speaks. So although the prophecy is not addressed to Babylon, it carries the conditional implications that regularly attach to prophecy. There is no need for judgment to fall if people respond to warnings.

In Isaiah 14:28-32 Yahweh reminds the Philistines that his afflicted people can find refuge in Zion, and also makes the point in more general terms: "The firstborn of poor people will pasture, the needy will lie down in safety." In the context of the trouble from Assyria that will threaten both Philistia and Judah, there is a hint that this offer is open to the Philistines.

The point is more evident in the Moab prophecy (Is 15:1–16:14). Yahweh joins in the lamenting at devastation that is coming on Moab and at the futility of its laborious efforts in prayer at its own sanctuary, and urges Moab to send an offering to Zion. He pictures the Moabites asking the Judahites for advice, seeking that Zion might become a shelter for Moabite survivors and acknowledging the authority and faithfulness of the one who sits on David's throne (Is 16:1-5). Perhaps talk of their making such a request is simply a sign of the extent of their devastation; but the implication is that they should be welcomed, if they come. Like the Moabites, the Sudanese "will bring tribute to Yahweh Armies . . . to the place of the name of Yahweh Armies, Mount Zion" (Is 18:7).

The "Damascus prophecy" (Is 17:1-11) concerns both Syria (Damascus being its capital) and Ephraim; these are the nations allied against Judah in Ahaz's day. There will only be remains left when Yahweh acts; but at least remains will be left. That fact can be a sign of hope, suggesting the possibility of a new beginning. The people who are left can look to their Maker.

The chapters' positive vision for the nations reaches its climax in Isaiah 19:18-25. While there is disaster to come for Egypt, there will also be Hebrew spoken in Egyptian cities and oaths taken in Yahweh's name there. They will include Sun-City, a place that was dedicated to the sun god. In the center of Egypt there will be an altar for offering sacrifice to Yahweh, and at Egypt's border a monument marking the country as belonging to Yahweh. Egypt will be able to cry out to Yahweh for help when it is oppressed, as the Israelites did when they were oppressed in Egypt (!), and Yahweh will deliver it as he delivered the Israelites from the Egyptians. Yahweh will thus make himself known to the Egyptians, and they will acknowledge him. They will experience chastisement but will turn back to Yahweh and find healing—again their experience will parallel Israel's. There will be a freeway between Egypt and Assyria via Israel that will facilitate peaceful relationships between the great powers to the north and to the south, and worship of Yahweh that they will share. (Is the reason why God chose Canaan as the location for his special people that it sits by the junction of Africa, Asia and Europe?) Israel will thus fulfill its vocation to be a blessing in the midst of the world—not because it can turn itself into a blessing, but because Yahweh will make it so. While Yahweh will still call Israel "my own possession," he will call Egypt "my people" and Assyria "my handiwork," descriptions that elsewhere apply only to Israel. Isaiah thus does not give up the idea of Israel's special significance but makes impossible any inference that Yahweh therefore does not care for other peoples.

Perhaps it is a bourgeois perspective that designates this vision as the climax of the prophecies' positive aspect. The prophecies close with the redeeming of Tyre's trading activity. Yes, it is whore's work, but Isaiah can see the whore's fees being set apart for Yahweh and supporting people who live before Yahweh.

The Whole Cosmos (Isaiah 24–27)

In chapters 24–27 the canvas broadens further still, to embrace the whole world, and indeed the entire cosmos, the heavens and the earth, supernatural as well as earthly powers, and a purpose that brings all things to their consummation. Once again the prophecies combine disaster and renewal, though with more explicit and systematic attention to renewal.

Isaiah 24–27 has been called "The Isaiah Apocalypse." An "apocalypse" is an account of a vision that reveals things that people could not know by ordinary means (which might cover heaven and hell, the future and the past, especially the end and the beginning of everything) and that couches its account in vivid imagery and symbolism. In its form Isaiah 24–27 is no more of an apocalypse, a visionary revelation, than other parts of the book. It does emphasize the coming of a decisive act of judgment, and it does use vivid symbolism. It takes up the experience of catastrophe that came to people and invites them to use their imagination in order to see disasters people have known as pointers to an even greater catastrophe.

LAND, CITY AND SUPERNATURAL POWERS

Isaiah 24 begins by declaring that a coming catastrophe will devastate the world as a whole. It will devastate the imperial capital, the great city (Is 25:1-5); one could think of Asshur or Nineveh or Babylon or Persepolis. One could also think of the hapless Moabites (Is 25:10-12). The catastrophe will affect not only the heavens and the earth but the cosmic powers. "On that day Yahweh will attend to the army on high" as well as the kings of earth (Is 24:21; see further Is 24:22-23). There are two stages to Yahweh's action. First these powers are put into captivity, presumably so as no longer to exercise their power. Then in due course they are actually "attended to." This verb (*pāqad*) is usually rendered "punish" in modern translations, but its meaning is more neutral than this rendering implies; the traditional translation "visit" is usefully redolent of a visit from the mafia. When the prophecy adds that "the moon will feel shamed, the sun will feel disgrace," the background is the way the heavenly bodies can be associated with the army on high. It was through the heavenly bodies that the gods ruled the earth.

Subsequently Isaiah 27:1 declares that Yahweh will in particular "attend to Leviathan the fleeing serpent, Leviathan the twisting serpent, and will slay the dragon that is in the sea." Leviathan is a figure that embodies dynamic power asserted against God. In effect, Leviathan is an Old Testament way of referring to the being called Satan in later Jewish writings and in the New Testament (compare the equation in Rev 12:9). We have noted that Isaiah speaks of a coming king of Israel but doesn't use the word *māšîaḥ* to refer to him, only to King Cyrus, and that elsewhere *māšîaḥ* is used only of a present king and a present priest. In a parallel way, the Old Testament does speak of an individual embodiment of dynamic power asserted against God, but doesn't use the word *sāṭān* to refer to him; when it uses the word *sāṭān,* it has other meanings.

Like other parts of both Old and New Testaments, then, Isaiah thus refers from time to time to supernatural entities that embody resistance to God, either plural or singular, without having consistent terminology for them or providing us with enough material to form a systematic picture. They simply constitute a recognition that resistance to God is not merely a human and this-worldly reality. The passages also offer an assurance that God has such resistance under control and will ultimately overwhelm it.

As was the case in the prophecies about individual nations, these chapters concentrate more on the fact of disaster than on its reasons, but they do explain that

> The earth was profane under its inhabitants,
> because they transgressed the teachings.
> They violated the statute,
> broke the age-old covenant.
> Therefore an oath has consumed the earth;
> the people who live in it have paid the penalty. (Is 24:5-6)

The presupposition is that the world as a whole had a covenant relationship with God that imposed rules of conduct for its behavior, which it has broken. The covenant the passage refers to is not a covenant commitment made by God to the world but one expected of the world by God. It is thus not like God's covenant with Noah, which was a commitment on God's part. It does parallel the idea that there were obligations God expected of the humanity that began with Noah, though these are obligations not elsewhere referred to as a covenant. They imply a similar assumption to the one Isaiah implied in connection with Assyria (Is 10:5-19). By virtue of being created by God, the world knows how to live and is under obligation to live that way, but it has declined. It has thus "profaned" the earth, made it something God no longer wishes to have anything to do with, something God could not continue to have anything to do with without compromising who he is. Links with Noah and the opening chapters of Genesis extend to the idea that the world had been under a curse but that God would never again doom the earth in the way he did at the flood. Perhaps humanity's failure to keep the expectations attached to the covenant mean that God feels free not to stick by that "never again."

THE CELEBRATION OF LIFE

When a city, a family or an individual experienced the kind of deliverance to which a psalm of thanksgiving relates, it would naturally have a great celebration. One can picture the family coming to the temple courtyards, bringing its thanksgiving sacrifice and sharing in a festive meal with God. The prophecy uses this practice as an image for picturing the celebration that will follow God's final act of deliverance from oppression (Is 25:6-8). The banquet will celebrate the fact that death and mourning have been terminated. The context makes clear that the idea is not that the shape of ordinary human life will have changed. In the new Jerusalem, the cessation of weeping and outcry does not mean there being no more dying at the end of a long life (Is 65:19-20). In Isaiah as elsewhere in the Old Testament, the reality of dying at the end of a long life is accepted. The Old Testament does rage when people cannot live out their lives because of other people's violence or duplicity. It is such violent death that Isaiah 25 promises will come to an end.

The motif of death and new life recurs in Isaiah 26:12-21. From the beginning, Israel had known itself ruled by foreign masters. There were the Egyptians and the Philistines, and then those imperial powers—Assyria, Babylon, Persia. But the present generation can look back on a sequence of such masters and note that they are now dead and gone. Ghosts don't rise from the dead. To underline the poignancy of death as the Old Testament sees it, God has not only "attended" to them (that verb recurs) and wiped them out; whereas people like to leave a legacy behind them so that they are remembered, Yahweh has even destroyed the memory of these peoples. The prophecy doesn't name these masters, ensuring that it doesn't unwittingly make its own statement deconstruct.

In contrast, whereas Judah is unable to give birth to a new future, God can do so. "Your dead will live, my corpse will rise," the prophet confesses. As usual the prophecy speaks not of individuals coming back to life but of the nation's rebirth, in the manner of the dry bones vision in Ezekiel 37. The chapter does make one comment on the destiny of Israelites who have died. When Yahweh attends to the world's wickedness, "the earth will disclose the blood shed on it, and will no longer hide its slain" (Is 26:21). Whereas Abel's blood cried out to God, and God heard the cry, it's now as if the soil has covered the blood of the people slain by Israel's overlords. The cover-up will not last forever.

The prophecy pictures the nation's resurrection in another way by commissioning a song about a vineyard that produces fruit (Is 27:2-6). It's a powerful image because Isaiah long ago described Israel as a vineyard that failed to produce fruit and that paid a terrible price (Is 5:1-7).

The Appropriate Response(s)

Among their declarations about the future, the chapters interweave a sequence of songs of praise to sing "in that day."

world devastation	24:1-13
response	24:14-16
cosmic devastation	24:17-23
response	25:1-5
world renewal and judgment	25:6-12
response	26:1-18
world renewal and judgment	26:19–27:13

Figure 2.3

The hymns interwoven into the prophecies suggest the appropriate response to the prophecies and the events they speak of. While such Old Testament hymns of praise are commonly responses to who God is or to what God has done for Israel in the past, they can also offer praise for what God intends to do. These particular hymns portray the worship that will be offered "on that day," when the events take place; they thereby implicitly suggest the response that is appropriate in anticipation of that day.

The first short section of response (Is 24:14-16) suggests two reactions to the first vision of disaster. The prophet hears voices shouting their recognition of Yahweh's majesty and urging the whole world to join in. Perhaps they are the voices of the survivors of the catastrophe; one way or another, evidently the destruction of the world that is portrayed in the vision doesn't mean all life has been destroyed. Forces that resist God are gone, and other people can rejoice in their deliverance from these forces and in the way God is now shown to be God. The prophet, however, is unable to join this exultation, overwhelmed by the picture of devastation and by the faithlessness that led to it, which is the continuing reality of the present.

The second song of praise (Is 25:1-5) is more unequivocal. It simply rejoices in the destruction of the foreign city. It speaks in the manner of a thanksgiving psalm of the kind that belongs in a celebration, as an individual or a community gives praise after experiencing God's act of deliverance from oppression or attack. While one point about such praise is to glorify God, the other aim is to give testimony to other people and thereby build up their trust in God. When the song is giving testimony to what God is going to do and speaking of the way God will have proved to be a refuge for the needy in their trouble and their vulnerability to the violent, it is thus bringing encouragement to these people who are at the moment still in trouble and under oppression from the violent. On that day they will be able to speak of the way they waited for Yahweh and experienced his deliverance, and now rejoice in it (Is 25:9); such a picture of what they will do functions to encourage people hearing the prophecy to trust and take the attitude of hope now.

The third song (Is 26:1-19) is the most extensive. It is equivocal in a different way from Isaiah 24:14-16. Declarations of trust alternate with implicit protests in relation to these statements of trust (for instance, that Yahweh brings the towering city down to the ground). The problem is that the statements are not vindicated by events. The city still stands. All that people can do is wait for Yahweh to act. But in the meantime, the faithless do well and the world as a whole is therefore not exactly encouraged to live faithfully. It's easy to feel like a pregnant woman who comes to term and gives birth to nothing—it was a phantom pregnancy. The song approaches its close with the declaration of confidence already noted. It is addressed to God, "Your dead will live, my corpse will rise," and buttressed by the further statement of trust, "because your dew is the dew of the lights." The community is like a corpse, but things won't end there. The song actually closes with an exhortation to the people, such as a prophet might sometimes respond to people's prayer and statement of trust. In view of the fact that God is indeed about to act, people will be well advised to hide to make sure they aren't caught by the backdraft of Yahweh's burning fury.

3

Isaiah 28–39

W*hen we turn on from Isaiah 27 to Isaiah 28,* we find ourselves back in the kind of prophecies and stories that appeared in chapters 1–12. The focus has narrowed back to Judah and Ephraim, to Jerusalem as David's city and to Judah's political policies. The difference over against chapters 1–12 is that there Isaiah was dealing with King Ahaz, and the political situation was dominated by the pressure that Syria and Ephraim put on Judah to join them in resisting Assyria. Isaiah is now dealing with Ahaz's son and successor King Hezekiah. Given that it was customary for a king to appoint his successor and make him co-ruler during his own reign, Hezekiah's reign likely overlapped with his father's (Ahaz reigned maybe 735–715, Hezekiah maybe 725–687). It was during his early years that the fears of Syria and Ephraim were realized, and they were overrun by the Assyrians. In the row of dominoes Judah is next in line, which is the dominant factor in the political situation for Hezekiah. In the time of Ahaz, Assyria was Judah's potential savior. Now it is Judah's potential conqueror, as Isaiah had already warned would happen. It is Egypt that is now the potential savior.

This collage has three sections, outlined opposite.

Like Isaiah 1–12, it has a complex arrangement. Section (a) could easily form the end of the book called Isaiah. Isaiah 33 takes up many of the themes of the first half of the book and rounds it off.[1] Yet section (a) also leads neatly

---

[1] 1QIs[a], the most complete Qumran scroll of Isaiah, leaves a space after chapter 33, as if to recognize this fact.

enough into section (b). The book called Isaiah could easily end there, too, with this vision of the ultimate consummation of Yahweh's purpose. In the book of Isaiah as a whole, however, section (b) functions to preview the themes of Isaiah 40–66, where there will be more talk of calamity involving Edom, of the transformation of the wilderness, of a new highway and of restoration for Judah. One might then have expected Isaiah 34–35 to lead straight into 40–66. But in fact, section (c) intervenes and takes us back to the circumstances to which section (a) relates, the Assyrian threat in the time of Hezekiah; one might thus have expected section (c) to follow section (a). Further, we have just noted that Isaiah 39 leads appropriately into Isaiah 40. The effect of the arrangement of Isaiah 28–39 is thus to tie closely together this collage and the one that follows (and thus to tie closely together Isaiah 1–39 and 40–66). Isaiah 34–35 looks forward as well as backward; Isaiah 36–39 looks backward as well as forward. Sections (b) and (c) form a pair of interwoven hooks between Isaiah 1–33 and Isaiah 40–66.

Chapters 28–33: five collections of prophecies that all begin with a "Hey" addressed to the people or the places involved in the present crisis (translations sometimes have words such as "Woe to" or "Alas for," but the term is mainly an attention getter). The prophecies combine threats and reassurances, with the threats dominating near the beginning of the sequence and the reassurances dominating near the end. They mostly date from about 711–700.

Chapters 34–35: a double declaration concerning calamity and renewal that looks way beyond this present crisis.

Chapters 36–39: a series of stories about Hezekiah and Isaiah. They appear in 2 Kings 18–20 as part of the story of the period. In Isaiah they further illustrate the theological issues that are important for Isaiah such as trust in Yahweh. They end up with the prospect of Hezekiah's descendants being taken off to Babylon, which enables them to form a bridge into the prophecies in chapters 40–55 where that prospect has been fulfilled.

Figure 3.1

Life and Death, Truth and Lies, Insight and Stupidity

Isaiah has a comprehensively different perspective on politics from his contemporaries. They sincerely believe they are pursuing the best policies for Judah. They know that Assyria is a great danger. It threatens the death of the nation. If Judah is to be preserved alive, the wise policy is an alliance with Egypt, the great power to the south, which will deliver protection.

Isaiah knows that this policy is misguided at every point. Judah's leaders have made an alliance or a covenant with death, not with life (Is 28:15). Part of the background to this phrase may be the Egyptians' well-known preoccupation with death and the afterlife, of which the pyramids are a symbol. Another part of the background may be the fact that Egypt had a prominent goddess called Mut, whose name was conveniently similar to the Hebrew word for death, *mot,* and thus to the name of the Canaanite death god, Mot.

The Judahites are thus treating something that is false and empty as if it could be a refuge, shelter, protection or source of help (Is 28:15; 30:2-3). The use of these words makes for a telling contrast with Psalm 91, which describes Yahweh as refuge, shelter, protection, source of help and object of trust. Judah is sending envoys off on a hazardous and costly mission to Egypt, but the mission will be futile (Is 30:6-7). Isaiah here neatly calls Egypt "Rahab sitting down." Rahab is another name for the monster also known as Leviathan (Is 27:1), the embodiment of dynamic power asserted against God (the name is different from that of the Rahab in Joshua, which is spelled differently in Hebrew). Rahab is a poetic term for Egypt in Psalm 87:4. But this so-called Rahab is like a monster that has gone to sleep, or like Leviathan reduced to a pet monster (Ps 104:26). Rahab/Egypt is going to be of no use to Judah.

In a particularly effective formulation, "Egypt is human not God, their horses are flesh not spirit" (Is 31:3). In the Old Testament, "flesh" does not carry the connotation of sinful, as it does in Paul; it simply designates human beings and animals as characterized by the weakness that attaches to something created, which does not carry dynamic life in itself. Conversely, "spirit" denotes the dynamism and power that is characteristic of God and can be shared by God with created beings, yet does not exactly become their possession. How foolish, then, for people to rely on human beings and animals rather than on God.

Judah's leaders think that their policies are so wise; they don't recognize that Yahweh's policy making is so much more insightful than theirs (Is 28:29). They go through the motions of being committed to Yahweh and submitting themselves to Yahweh, and they go to the temple to pray for Yahweh's help and to seek Yahweh's guidance, but once they are back in the palace they formulate their policies on the basis of their own so-called insight (Is 29:13-14), in the way that Christian meetings usually work. They might necessarily be secretive in formulating their policies in connection with making an alliance with Egypt; Isaiah's comment about secretiveness (Is 29:15) is paralleled by the desire attributed to Hezekiah's staff that the Assyrian field commander should shout his message to them in Aramaic rather than in Hebrew so that the ordinary Jerusalemites can't understand (Is 36:11). But the confidential nature of these proceedings would then make for a contrast with what went on when they all went to the temple. Without realizing it, they're like clay telling the potter that they know more about pottery than he does and that they can form themselves into pots on their own (Is 29:16). Without realizing it, they are like people telling their prophets to shut up, or at least to give the people encouragement in their needy situation rather than always being negative. Without realizing it, they want the prophets to stop talking about Israel's Holy One. They want a more encouraging God (Is 30:10-11). It's as if Yahweh has made them unable to see sense (as Is 6:9-10 said), and specifically as if he has deprived the prophets and seers of their capacity to see, or rendered them unable to read plain truth (Is 29:9-12).

Once again Isaiah is to write his message down so that it may be shown to have been right when it comes true (Is 30:8).

Yahweh's Dilemma

Isaiah earlier described Assyria as Yahweh's angry club (Is 10:5). In other words, Assyria wields the club with which it knocks Judah down, but in doing so it is the executor of Yahweh's anger. Yahweh's capacity for anger is a sign of his being a personal being. One of the characteristics of a person is having a range of emotions. Isaiah had already declared that Yahweh's passion (*qînâ*) is the key factor in seeing that he will indeed replace darkness by light in Israel's experience (Is 9:7 [6]). Yahweh is a fully personal being with all the strong feelings that go with being personal: love, compassion, tenderness, joy, grief, hatred, fury. The Old Testament does not divide such emotions into ones that are inherently good and ones that are inherently bad. Each emotion can be appropriate or inappropriate according to the circumstances. Yet there are emotions that come more naturally to Yahweh in his relationship with Israel, and ones that come less naturally. In this collage, the way Isaiah expresses that point is by describing Yahweh's expression of anger as a strange action on Yahweh's part (Is 28:21-22). Yahweh can be wrathful, but it doesn't come as instinctively as the expression of faithfulness and mercy. It is foreign to Yahweh to act against his people, but he is prepared to undertake this alien action when necessary.

Yahweh is caught by the tension between needing to be faithful to Judah and to Jerusalem because of a commitment made to them, and needing not to treat their waywardness as something trivial. In both respects he has to be faithful to himself and also to avoid making himself look stupid.

One way of squaring this circle was to let enemies attack Jerusalem, cause considerable trouble there, and almost capture it, but then to deliver it at the last minute. In picturing things in this way, in Isaiah 29:1-8 Yahweh starts from the presence of an altar hearth (*'ărî'ēl*) in the temple courtyard in Jerusalem. The hearth surrounded the altar where sacrifices were burned. Yahweh turns that word into a name for Jerusalem itself. It's like a hearth around the temple. But Yahweh is going to bring attackers to Jerusalem—that is, the forces of Assyria itself. At Isaiah 13:3 he described the Medians as his army, the troops he sanctified as his warriors; here he declares that he himself will encamp against Jerusalem the way David once did. The trouble is that the Jerusalemites are now in the position of the Jebusites back then. It will be as if the city and the temple are an altar and its hearth, and as if they are themselves consumed by the fire on the altar. The people who were trying to avoid death will be near death (Is 29:4). But then, at the last minute, Yahweh will change sides and blow the attackers away. To put it in different imagery (Is 31:4-5), Yahweh is a lion or a hawk hovering over Jerusalem, and Jerusalem is its victim. A whole gang of shepherds is not going to be able to deprive the lion of its prey. But then the lion or the hawk turns into the protector, one who keeps the "prey" safe from other attackers. The account of Sennacherib's campaign in Judah in the story in Isaiah 36–37 implies the same picture and the same theology.

In his own annals relating to about the year 701, the Assyrian King Sennacherib records:

> As for Hezekiah, the Judahite, who had not submitted to my yoke, 46 of his fortified cities I besieged and captured, along with many smaller towns. . . . As for him, I shut him up like a caged bird in his royal city of Jerusalem. I constructed a series of fortresses around him.[2]

Sennacherib's account corresponds to the narrative in Isaiah 36–37, though that narrative puts a different spin on "shut him up like a caged bird" by implying "but didn't manage to take Jerusalem." Isaiah's prophetic response to Hezekiah's prayer in the midst of that crisis promised that the city will escape and that "leftovers will come out of Jerusalem." Sennacherib will not enter the city because Yahweh will defend it and deliver it "for my sake and for the sake of David my servant" (Is 37:32-35). The story goes on to relate how Yahweh does so in fulfillment of Isaiah's declarations.

Another way Yahweh can square the circle is by getting the adversaries actually to take the city and destroy it, but then restoring it (Is 29:17-24). In that connection the prophecy also speaks of the necessary reversal of the imposition of deafness and blindness on the people, of how the oppressors will disappear and the oppressed will be restored, and of how Yahweh will be acknowledged in reality and not merely in words. For the time being, then, "Yahweh waits to be gracious to you; but therefore he will arise to show compassion to you"; in the meantime, it will be the people's job to "wait for him" when they experience "trouble bread and affliction water" (Is 30:18, 20). Then

---

[2]Adapted from the translation in D. D. Luckenbill, *The Annals of Sennacherib* (Chicago: University of Chicago Press, 1924), p. 70.

Yahweh will be willing to speak to them again in a way that they can hear; then Yahweh will bind up their wounds; then he will put Assyria down (Is 30:21-33).

Reversal and Restoration

The two aspects of reversal and restoration are spelled out in Isaiah 34–35, following on the "Hey, you" chapters. They speak of destruction for the nations (Is 34:1-17) and transformation for the people whom Yahweh intends to "restore" or "redeem" (Is 35:1-10).

The first of these verbs is *gā'al.* Its participle, *gō'ēl,* is itself commonly rendered "redeemer," and this translation does convey some aspects of the word's meaning; a *gō'ēl* is a man (it would be bound to be a man in that cultural context) who has resources that he is willing to expend on behalf of a person in need. But it is of the essence of the idea of a *gō'ēl* that the person who extends these resources does so on the basis of a family relationship that the *gō'ēl* and the needy person share. Because they belong to the same extended family, the *gō'ēl* is someone under moral obligation to use those resources to restore the position of the needy person to what it should be. Applying the verb *gā'al* to Yahweh or designating Yahweh as Israel's *gō'ēl,* then, designates Israel as a member of Yahweh's family to whom Yahweh accepts this family obligation. If the Israelites are people "restored" by Yahweh, they are people to whom Yahweh has behaved in this way. But one common way in which a restorer would need to act would be to rescue someone from servitude that had come about through debt, or was threatened by debt, and this connection explains the implication "redeem." In Isaiah 35, the second verb, *pādâ,* is again implicitly a word from family relationships, but it more indicates the expenditure of resources. In Numbers 18, for instance, it refers to the payment of five sheqels to "redeem" the firstborn offspring of human beings and animals that are owed to God.

The motif that Isaiah 34 and 35 have in common is "redress" (Is 34:8; 35:4). They presuppose a logic that has obtained earlier in Isaiah. It's all very well to harness the nations' instinct to self-aggrandizement and violence as a means of bringing disaster to Israel when it deserves it, but matters can hardly be left there. It's surely necessary to restore Israel, and it's surely also necessary to require the nations to pay their penalty. The word for redress, *nāqām,* is often translated "vengeance," but this translation gives a misleading impression. While the emotional connotations of "vengeance" are not foreign to Yahweh's action, in English "vengeance" or "revenge" easily implies action in which such personal feelings are dominant and excessive; *nāqām* suggests a punishment that fits the crime.

The particular focus on Edom in Isaiah 34 fits with the theme of restoration following calamity for Judah. Other prophets imply that the Edomites supported the Babylonians when they laid siege to Jerusalem and took the city, and that they then took advantage of the Judahites' defeat (see, e.g., Ezek 35). In addition, in the Second Temple period the Edomites gradually took over much of southern Judah. So it is not surprising that a promise that Yahweh would restore Judah would say something about Edom. What happened in due course was that the Edomites (or Idumeans, as they were later called) were converted to Judaism rather than being annihilated, which shows once more that Yahweh is willing to be flexible about the fulfillment of his words. At the same time, it may have been the significance of Edom as a major encroacher on Judah's territory that contributed to Edom's becoming a symbol for a hostile power, like Babylon; in the Targum, Edom is a figure for Rome. Perhaps that significance already obtains in Isaiah 34.

Trust (Again)

In Hezekiah's reign, the key issues in Judah's life remain as they were earlier. Centrally, the question is: Will the people live by trust in the promise of God regarding king and city, treating these promises as the key to their security and freedom, or will they rather insist on seeking freedom and security in alliances with stronger nations?

The idea of making trust in God the basis of your political policies seems ridiculously naive to Isaiah's contemporaries, including other prophets and priests (Is 28:9-13). But strength lies in quiet trust, Yahweh declares (Is 30:15). While the implication of Isaiah 28–33 is thus that the Judahite leadership has a hard time operating on this basis, the stories in Isaiah 36–37 portray Hezekiah as willing to do so.

Isaiah 36 has Sennacherib's field commander challenging Hezekiah's staff about the wisdom of relying either on Egyptian support or on Yahweh. But ironically, he has undermined Sennacherib's position by ridiculing Yahweh's capacity to keep Jerusalem from being captured (Is 37:1-4). The narrative later reports Sennacherib himself also ridiculing the idea that Yahweh can protect Jerusalem from capture, in a letter to Hezekiah. Fortunately Hezekiah knows that Sennacherib has thus made a fatal mistake, and can appeal to Yahweh accordingly (Is 37:9-20). Each time Isaiah's response picks up the motif of Sennacherib's slight of Yahweh (Is 37:6, 22-29).

We have noted that the prophecies in Isaiah 28–31 imply that Hezekiah had difficulty trusting in Yahweh, while the narrative in Isaiah 36–37 portrays him as a man of trust. The ambiguity in the account of Hezekiah continues in the closing stories in the collage in Isaiah 38–39. Oddly, one might think, he finds trust easier in connection with politics than he does in connection with his personal life, where the stories are more equivocal. When he is mortally sick he prays for healing. God responds, and also God gives him a sign that his healing will come. Why does God give him the sign? At the very end, the chapter whispers, "Hezekiah had asked for a sign." Yet his father had been right, though for the wrong reasons; ideally, we aren't supposed to ask for signs (Is 7:12). Hezekiah has done so, and Yahweh has responded.

The final story describes a visit from some Babylonian envoys. These are the Babylonians of Isaiah and Hezekiah's day, living in the shadow of Assyria like Judah itself and seeking alliance with Judah in rebelling against Assyrian authority. Hezekiah lets them see all the resources he has, which will enable them to know what kind of alliance it is worth making with Judah; at this point, at least, he is not obviously making trust the basis of his political policies. He thereby earns Isaiah's rebuke and receives a warning that the Babylonians themselves will end up appropriating all these resources. His story closes with his expressing appreciation for the fact that well-being will reliably continue in his own day (Is 39:8). Perhaps the reflection is less cynical than it sounds, in that it signifies that Yahweh will continue to have mercy on Judah, will not treat it as it deserves and will postpone judgment, but Hezekiah's story does end in ambiguity.

4

Isaiah 40–55

We have noted that Isaiah 39 leads neatly into Isaiah 40 by means of its reference to the way Judah's leadership and its resources will end up in Babylon. But Isaiah 40 leapfrogs over the intervening history of Judah between Isaiah's day and the fall of Jerusalem, and over the decades of exile itself, and addresses the Judahite community on the eve of Babylon's own fall. Here are some key dates:

700s	The last scenes in Isaiah's ministry
597	The first fall of Jerusalem (Ezekiel and others exiled)
587	The second fall of Jerusalem (many others exiled)
540s	The rise of Cyrus the Persian
539	The fall of Babylon to Cyrus (Judahites free to go home)

Figure 4.1

It's usually assumed that the Judahites addressed by the prophecy are exiles in Babylon, but the chapters are not explicit on the point. They talk both about Babylon and about Jerusalem; Babylon would be important to Judahites in Jerusalem, and Jerusalem would be important to Judahites in Babylon.

This fourth collage is the one that is unequivocally linear. It might be outlined as follows.

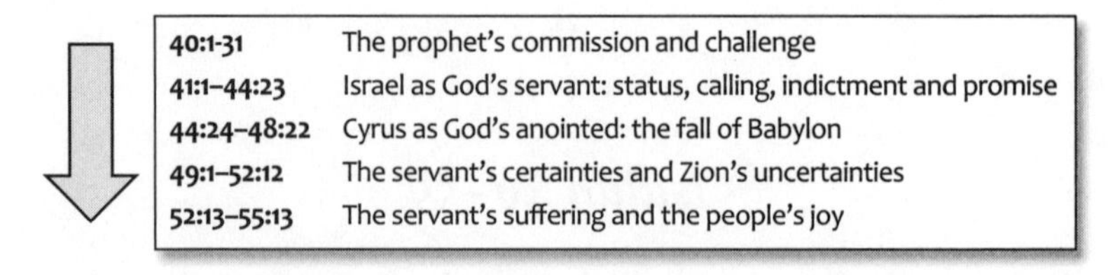

40:1-31	The prophet's commission and challenge
41:1–44:23	Israel as God's servant: status, calling, indictment and promise
44:24–48:22	Cyrus as God's anointed: the fall of Babylon
49:1–52:12	The servant's certainties and Zion's uncertainties
52:13–55:13	The servant's suffering and the people's joy

Figure 4.2

YAHWEH ALONE IS GOD

This fourth collage has a distinctively robust understanding of God. Toward the end of the second of the two introductions that open the collage, the prophecy declares that "Yahweh is the eternal God, creator of earth's ends" (Is 40:28). As creator of the ends of the earth, Yahweh is of course also creator of everything that lies between. He is creator of earth from end to end. He is also the eternal God—literally, "the God of the age." Yahweh is the one who has always been God, even back to creation. The description does not imply that Yahweh is timeless or outside time but that he is present to all time and unlimited by time. The parallel with the statement about being creator of earth's ends perhaps makes it appropriate to infer that being the God of the age means Yahweh is God from the beginning to the end, and for all the time in between.

The declaration spells out the implications of statements the prophecy has made in the paragraphs that led up to it (Is 40:12-26). God created the world, and he needed no help in doing so. An image cannot represent who he is. He sits all-powerful over the cosmos. He is sovereign over the so-called cosmic powers represented by the planets and stars. The implication is that he alone is God. A simple consideration of the process whereby images are made shows how a god who can be represented by an image cannot be compared with Yahweh (Is 44:9-20). The point is unaffected by the fact that a sophisticated person who uses images in worship distinguishes between the image and the god it represents. If the static, humanly made image can represent the god in any way, it's not much of a god. To put the point even more pungently, the problem with these gods is that one has to carry them, in the sense of carrying their images. The real God is one who carries his people (Is 46:1-7).

It can be said that Isaiah 40–55 offers the clearest articulation of monotheism in the Old Testament. Yet this formulation sets the prophecy's own declarations in a different framework from its own. Its point is not that there is only one God as opposed to there being two or three or six or a hundred. It is that Yahweh alone is God. There are many other supernatural beings in existence, but they don't deserve to be honored by the designation "God" even though we might call them gods with a small *g* (or one could think of them as spirits or demons or angels). Isaiah is not concerned so much with how many gods there are (the monotheism-polytheism question) as with the question of who is God. The basis for the initial declaration that Yahweh alone is God is the nature of creation. The prophecy does not seek to prove that Yahweh is God on this basis but to remind Judahites that this is what they believe: "Don't you acknowledge, or haven't you listened?" (Is 40:28). It knows that the Judahites acknowledge the facts about Yahweh in theory. The problem is that they don't carry over their nominal faith into the way they look at everyday life and at the current political situation.

What is the evidence that Yahweh is the only one who really deserves the designation "God"? It comes from historical and political events. It does so in two ways. First, the prophecy points to the arousing of someone from the east (Is 41:1-4)—the description fits both Abraham, the Judahites' ancestor, and Cyrus, the Persian conqueror of the Babylonian empire. Who aroused these figures? Not a Babylonian deity, in either case. The arousing is evidence for Yahweh's self-declaration, "I am Yahweh, the first, and I am the one, with the last." Or as Yahweh later puts it, "I am the first and I am the last;" in fact, "apart from me there is no god" (Is 44:6).

The prophecy provides the second piece of evidence when it adds force to the question about who aroused the figures from the east, by asking who announced these events ahead of time, or can give an account of them, or can say where they will lead. Again, neither Babylonian gods nor their representatives did so or can do so, whereas Yahweh has done so through the messengers he has given Judah (Is 41:21-29). "Who like me proclaims and announces it?" (Is 44:7). The idea is not merely that Yahweh has unparalleled ability to foretell what is going to happen, though that is so. It is that Yahweh's capacity to declare what is going to happen stems from and evidences the fact that Yahweh is the one who determines what is going to happen. Thus Babylon may have all the information resources in the world, but they will do Babylon no good because they don't access Yahweh's intentions in the way the Israelite prophets do (Is 47:8-15).

Israel Is Yahweh's Servant and Witness

In the midst of the crisis brought on by the way Cyrus is turning the political situation upside down in the 540s, the Judahites are tempted to be as panicked as the Babylonians. They ought not to have that reaction, because they are the servant of the God who is making events happen (Is 41:8-16).

The previous collage referred to David as Yahweh's servant (Is 37:35); the collage before that one referred to Isaiah ben Amoz himself and to Eliakim in this way (Is 20:3; 22:20). In each case a servant is someone committed to his master but also someone to whom his master is committed. It's a mutual relationship. Isaiah ben Amoz declared that Yahweh would protect Jerusalem for the sake of his servant David. Here the prophecy turns the master-servant relationship between Yahweh and David into a figure for the relationship between Yahweh and Israel. It is the reason why Israel ought not to be in the state of panic that justifiably afflicts the Babylonians. As was the case with David, being Yahweh's servant means Israel has Yahweh's commitment to it.

Over the centuries before the exile, Yahweh would have been quite justified in throwing out this servant because of its shortcomings, but he has not done so. On the contrary, "Israel's Holy One is your restorer" (Is 41:14). In earlier collages, Yahweh's being Israel's Holy One was the reason it had to be disciplined for those shortcomings. This collage turns that argument on its head. Yahweh's being Israel's Holy One is also the reason why Yahweh cannot simply throw off Israel. He has made a commitment that he cannot get out of, even when Israel fails to live up to its side of the commitment. So he will act as Israel's restorer. Isaiah 41 takes up the image of Yahweh as Israel's *gō'ēl,* trailered in the use of the verb *gā'al* in Isaiah 35:10. Israel is a member of Yahweh's family, to whom Yahweh accepts this family obligation.

Of course being a servant does imply obligation as well as security. Thus Yahweh goes on to describe the work that his servant is expected to do (Is 42:1-4). His servant is one who will let the nations know of the sovereign purpose in history that he has been pursuing, the sovereign purpose of which Abraham and Cyrus were both part. They will thus come to know about *mišpāṭ*: the word comes three times in the prescription. It is a word that played a key part at the beginning of the book, where it referred to the proper exercise of power and authority in Israel ("justice" is the conventional translation, but it gets at only part of the significance of the word). Here it refers to Yahweh's exercise of power and authority, the way Yahweh is involved in making decisions in the world. No one can make sense of the political situation; the job of Yahweh's servant is to explain what Yahweh is doing, explain how it fits into a constructive purpose.

The nations are waiting to know about such a purpose. So Yahweh took hold of Israel with the intention of making it into "a covenant for the people, a light for the nations" (Is 42:6). In other words, the covenant relationship between Yahweh and Israel and the way Yahweh shone his light of blessing in Israel's life was designed to become a revelation to other peoples, a means of opening their eyes and releasing them from darkness.

This declaration must make readers uneasy, because the description of the servant's role doesn't look like one that Israel can fulfill. Readers already know that Israel is blind and in captivity. It doesn't understand the way Yahweh is involved in bringing about his purpose. The unease is confirmed when the prophecy goes on to urge deaf people to listen and blind people to see, and then to ask, "Who is blind except my servant, and as deaf as my aide, whom I send?" (Is 42:19). The prophecy thus picks up a motif from the first collage: Yahweh threatened to make Israel deaf and blind, and he has done so (Is 6:9-10). But a deaf and blind servant is itself in need of a servant's ministry. It cannot exercise that ministry.

It would again be natural for the master therefore to throw the servant out, but the prophecy continues to presuppose what we have called Yahweh's dilemma. Yahweh has made a commitment he cannot get out of. Yahweh is, after all, the one who created and shaped Israel, and he is therefore committed to being the one who will restore it and declare ownership of it. At the beginning of its story he declined to pursue any claim over Egypt but took hold of Israel, and he intends to continue this policy (Is 43:1-7). Paradoxically, precisely by ignoring Israel's inadequacies and rescuing it, he will turn it into a body of witnesses to who he is and what he can do; so it still has the position of Yahweh's servant (Is 43:8-13; 44:1-8). The fact that Yahweh's restoring of Israel is not at all based on what it deserves gives this action the potential to lead Israel itself into an acknowledgment of Yahweh. The idea is not that Israel returns to Yahweh and therefore Yahweh forgives it and restores it; it is rather that Yahweh forgives it and restores it, and this action must draw Israel to return to Yahweh (Is 44:21-22).

Cyrus My Shepherd, My Anointed

Isaiah ben Amoz has described Assyria as Yahweh's angry club, and although no one seems to have taken much notice at the time, as far as we know Isaiah didn't get into too much trouble for speaking in these terms. In the chronological gap between Isaiah 39 and Isaiah 40, Jeremiah has described the Babylonian king Nebuchadnezzar as Yahweh's servant, for which Jeremiah got into considerable trouble; he could have lost his life for such talk, were there not a precedent from Isaiah's day (see Jer 25–26). Isaiah 44:24–45:7 now describes Cyrus as Yahweh's shepherd and Yahweh's anointed. Although he does not recognize Yahweh at the moment, Yahweh's acting through him is designed to give him reason to do so.

In the Middle East, in Old Testament times, "shepherd" was a recognized way to describe the role of a king. A shepherd is in charge of his sheep both in terms of controlling them and of providing for them. Applied to a king, the image suggests both the holding of authority and the responsibility to protect the people. In the Old Testament it has not been used of

Israelite kings, but it is used of the new David whom Yahweh promises (Ezek 34:23; 37:24). Here, it is Cyrus who is Yahweh's shepherd, who will fulfill the Davidic role of commissioning the rebuilding of Jerusalem and of the temple. Cyrus is also Yahweh's *māšîaḥ;* we have noted that this term is used in the Old Testament of Israelite kings, but not of the new David concerning whom the prophets sometimes speak.

These parallels suggest that describing a foreign ruler as Yahweh's shepherd and as Yahweh's anointed, in connection with attributing to him a positive role in connection with Israel's destiny, would indeed raise eyebrows for Judahites. It would do so all the more for Judahites in Babylon who had settled down there and come to be identified with Babylon's fortunes. It would not be surprising if it provoked the negative reaction that the prophet goes on to relate (Is 45:9-13; 46:8-13). The prophet declares that Cyrus is to take David's place in relation to the fulfillment of Yahweh's promises to Israel. Doing so is designed not only to lead to Israel recognizing Yahweh and to Cyrus recognizing Yahweh but to the ends of the earth recognizing Yahweh as the one who has delivered them from Babylonian overlordship (Is 45:18-25).

Babylon's self-understanding is very much like the one Isaiah ben Amoz attributed to Assyria. It is proud of its majesty and its achievements in a way that is in some respects quite justified. The trouble is, in effect Ms. Babylon has thus come to see herself as God: "I shall always be here, mistress forever. . . . I and I alone am still here" (Is 47:7, 8). No superpower can ever imagine it will cease to be in power, but this means its pretension is quasi-divine and must be corrected.

In its own way, Israel is not so much better. All those declarations about divine faithfulness and grace do not in the short term alter Israel's attitudes (Is 48:1-15). With poignancy Yahweh declares, "If only you had attended to my commands" (Is 48:18). Then Israel could have enjoyed *šālôm.* The question is, is Israel yet ready to start taking notice of Yahweh's commands? Here is one such command: "Get ready to get out of Babylon." As Israel decides whether to heed the command, remember that to ignore Yahweh's commands makes one a rebel, and there is no *šālôm* for rebels (Is 48:20-22).

Yahweh's using Cyrus as his shepherd and his anointed, as a new David, thus solves one problem about Israel but leaves another unresolved. It was a problem for the fulfillment of Yahweh's purpose that Israel was in captivity; it was in no position to model the freedom and blessing that Israel was designed to model if it was to embody what it was like to have Yahweh in covenant relationship with a people and thus to make other peoples seek that relationship. Yahweh can solve that problem by means of Cyrus. But the reason why the people were in captivity was that they were deaf and blind to Yahweh, and they remain deaf and blind. They still cannot function as Yahweh's servant in that state. So where does Yahweh go from here?

A Prophet as Yahweh's Servant

A prophet's own person is often important in a prophetic book; the messenger and the message are interwoven. Thus Isaiah has appeared in the first collage (see Is 6:1–8:18), in the second (see Is 20:1-6) and in the third (see Is 36:1–39:8).

In this fourth collage, the prophet first features at the very beginning, where Yahweh commissions a proclamation. A voice responds to that commission by asking how it is possible to preach, when the people who are to receive the proclamation are in the same condition as grass that has been withered by the searing summer sun (Is 40:6-7). The Isaiah scroll from Qumran that we mentioned in connection with Isaiah 33, and also the Septuagint, makes explicit that it is the "I" of the prophet that makes this response, and the same implication likely holds in the Masoretic Text itself. This "I" surfaces explicitly in Isaiah 48:16, voicing an awareness of being sent with Yahweh's spirit. But at the beginning its response to Yahweh's commission is rather different from that of Isaiah ben Amoz, the volunteer (Is 6:8).

This prophetic "I" becomes more central in Isaiah 49:1-6. It is one of the passages that Bernhard Duhm called "servant songs" and saw as randomly inserted later additions to the text, but they are no more "songs" than other passages in the collage, and less so than some others. Duhm's theory about "servant songs" has been very popular, but it hasn't helped the interpretation of the text. It has simply made it impossible to interpret the passages when they have no context, whereas taking them as an intrinsic part of the collage opens up a coherent understanding. In his commentary on chapters 40–66, R. Norman Whybray noted that when prophets use the word "I" they regularly refer either to themselves or to God, and that the assumption that the prophet speaks of himself in Isaiah 49:1-6 and Isaiah 50:4-9 makes sense of both passages.[1]

Like Jeremiah, the prophet first speaks of being designated by Yahweh before he was born, and then speaks of being personally designated as Yahweh's servant. It is one of the ways in which he walks in the footsteps of Isaiah ben Amoz (see Is 20:3). Following on Isaiah 40:1–48:22, however, the designation as Yahweh's servant has a new import. Those preceding chapters have emphasized that Israel is Yahweh's servant, but that this servant is deaf and blind, yet that Yahweh is nevertheless still committed to keeping Israel as his servant and to using Israel as his servant. The question is, how is Yahweh to fulfill his purpose to use Israel as his servant?

The answer is that it will come about by Yahweh's using the prophet as his servant on an interim basis, in order to turn Israel into an entity that can itself be used in this way. The prophet is one person who is willing to give Yahweh the kind of response needed from a servant. He thus embodies what Israel is supposed to be. There is thus the possibility of using him to draw Israel to a proper response to Yahweh (Is 49:1-3).

The trouble is, Isaiah 40–48 implies that so far his attempt to draw people in this direction has been a spectacular failure, though through no fault of his. Pointing out this fact to Yahweh leads (with some irony) to Yahweh's increasing the dimensions of the task, or at least to pointing out that it has a dimension that the prophet may not have seen. The prophet is also going to be the means whereby news of Yahweh's deliverance comes to the nations (Is 49:4-6). In the only quotation from this passage in the New Testament, Paul applies this commission to the mission undertaken by himself and Barnabas (Acts 13:47). The fact that most people who read

[1]R. Norman Whybray, *Isaiah 40–66* (Grand Rapids: Eerdmans, 1981).

the book called Isaiah today are Gentiles shows how Yahweh's intention has been amply fulfilled.

The prophetic "I" reappears in Isaiah 50:4-9, where the prophet has to speak not only of a sense that his work is unsuccessful but of the experience of people abusing him and physically attacking him.[2] He is not explicit about whether his attackers are Babylonians or Israelites. One can imagine that either might feel they had reason to attack him. The message about Yahweh's intention to bring down the Babylonian empire would not endear him to Babylonians or to Judahites who identified with their rulers, while his critique of the Judahites would give them further reason for resentment. Yet he is convinced that Yahweh's plan to use him will be fulfilled. He will be vindicated.

In a postscript to this testimony (Is 50:10-11) he gives his listeners a challenge in this connection. They have to decide whom they are going to follow. They can be responsive to Yahweh and to his servant, and if necessary walk trustingly along the dark road he walks. In effect, the prophet is inviting people to join him in forming a faithful group within Israel that gives Yahweh his proper response—the kind of group that is often referred to as a faithful remnant (though the prophet does not use this language). Or they can stay with the people who are trying set him on fire. They will then find that the fire consumes them too.

AN OFFERING TO MAKE

A feature of this postscript is that the prophet moves to speaking of himself in the third person: "Who among you is in awe of Yahweh, listens to the voice of his servant?" (Is 50:10). He comes back to this third-person way of speaking in the most famous of the passages about Yahweh's servant: Isaiah 52:13–53:12. I assume, in other words, that he continues to speak about himself here, though the theological significance of the passage is not affected if it was written about him by someone else, or if it is his vision of some other unidentified person being attacked and vindicated.

---

[2]While there are many indications of an awareness of a woman's experience in these chapters, Isaiah 50:6 suggests that the prophet has a beard, so the pronoun "he" seems appropriate.

In this vision, Yahweh's servant has been attacked and is as good as dead, but the vision begins by declaring that this servant is going to be vindicated. The account of the rejection and persecution that has already happened goes over again what we know from the earlier testimonies but portrays it more vividly. The servant has been repudiated and attacked by people. They believed that he was being punished by God. He was a false prophet and he got what he deserved.

But they have now come to realize that this assessment must be wrong, and it seems that the key factor in this realization was the way he coped with their attacks—the fact that he did not attack them back. If he did not deserve the persecution that was being meted out to him, then one significance of what was happening was that he was suffering *with* them when he did not deserve to do so. They deserved to be in exile; he was a person like Jeremiah or Ezekiel, who had been faithful to Yahweh but shared in the suffering of exile when he did not deserve it. Another significance of what was happening was that he was suffering *for* them in the sense that he was paying the price for ministering to them, despite the fact that they attacked him.

But there was something else. He knew that they really needed to be able to make an offering to God to compensate for their unfaithfulness, but precisely because of their unfaithfulness, they had nothing to offer. But the fact that he didn't deserve his persecution yet was willing to accept it meant it might be a sort of offering he could make to God on their behalf. He could make himself, in his suffering, an offering to God on their behalf, instead of them. You might think that a single person's self-offering could hardly compensate for a whole people's rebellion, but the basis on which offerings worked was never that the offering was quantitatively equivalent (on the Day of Atonement a goat stood for the entire people). And one offering of commitment and self-sacrifice on the part of a member of the people might possibly compensate for the people's rebellion.

So he bore "the punishment that made us whole" (Is 53:5). The idea is thus not that God was a judge who was exacting a punishment from his servant instead of from the people. Possibly the idea is that the punishment that the Babylonians and/or Judahites meted out to him was what brought *šālôm* to them. But the word for "punishment" is not a word that is ever used for the action of a court. It is more a word that belongs in the context of family life (most of the occurrences are in Proverbs). It denotes chastisement or discipline. The servant was going through the kind of punishing regimen that is often involved in an athlete's training, not to make him fit but to make them fit. "It was because of my people's rebellion that the blow fell on him" (Is 53:8).

But that will not be the end of the story. In this vision the persecution has happened, and it looks as if it might be the end of the story; the prophet might simply die as a martyr. His grave has been allocated for him. But death will not be the end. He will either be delivered at the last minute or raised from death (there are a number of Old Testament stories about God raising someone from death, so this idea is not inconceivable). One way or the other he will then come to be recognized by the world as well as by his own people. The most striking description of this vindication is that he will receive an extraordinary anointing (Is 52:14).[3] Cyrus is anointed in recognition of his significance in the fulfillment of God's purpose. This servant is anointed in recognition of his parallel significance.

Isaiah 53 is not a prophecy of the Messiah but a portrait of how Yahweh's servant-prophet becomes the means of Israel's being put right with God, of Israel's personal renewal, and of the nations' coming to acknowledge Yahweh. But one can see how the chapter came to help people understand Jesus' significance. It is common to note that the atonement has an objective side and a subjective side—that is, it makes a difference to God and to us. The prophet's self-sacrifice has both aspects. The prophet reaches out to God with an offering on the people's behalf (on the basis of God's having given him the chance to do so). The prophet also reaches out to the people and to the world and draws them to acknowledge God.

[3]Translations usually take the verse to refer to his disfigurement, but even a non-Hebraist will be able to see similarities between *mišḥat* and *māšîaḥ*, and *mišḥat* never refers elsewhere to disfigurement and usually links with anointing.

The Transformed City and the Covenant People

It was a vision. In it the persecution has happened; the recognition has not yet happened. The promises that are interwoven with the testimonies of the prophet-servant continue to try to get the people to see the truth.

Jerusalem-Zion will be restored and transformed. At the moment it feels abandoned and forgotten. Initially Yahweh denies that either of these feelings corresponds to reality (Is 49:14–50:3). People who are looking for Yahweh to act in faithfulness to Zion need to look back to what Yahweh did with Abraham and Sarah (Is 51:1-8). Yahweh is commissioning his arm to take action again, but in a more positive fashion than when he stretched out his hand in judgment in the first collage (Is 51:9-16). Therefore Jerusalem is to get up out of the dirt and put on its glory clothes (Is 51:17–52:12).

"Ahem," Yahweh later says, however, "well, actually, yes, I did abandon you, but only momentarily, and the abandonment will fade into insignificance alongside the permanence of my renewed commitment to you" (Is 54:1-8). Once again Yahweh is handling the tension between the obligation to be faithful and the obligation to be disciplinary. He is expressing the tension in yet another slightly different way. The acknowledgment of abandonment leads into a more extravagant declaration of an eternal commitment for which God's covenant with Noah provides a model (Is 54:9-17), but it would be unwise to infer that this declaration somehow resolves this true tension. The reappearance of the tension in the final collage will confirm this point (as does subsequent history; God has indeed abandoned Jerusalem again, notably in A.D. 70).

Jacob-Israel will be restored and transformed. It will fulfill its vocation to be "a covenant for the people" (Is 49:8)—that is, the world's people (as in Is 42:6). That vocation has not been taken away from it; God's involvement with the prophet-servant is only an interim arrangement. Precisely in restoring Jacob-Israel, Yahweh will shine a light on the nations. In a striking formulation, Yahweh finally speaks of the lot that will be enjoyed by his servants—plural (Is 54:17). That plural will also recur in the final collage.

The nature of Jacob-Israel's position is spelled out in Isaiah 55:3-5. Once again Yahweh speaks in terms of a covenant, and for the only time in this collage he explicitly refers to David. He intends to conclude for the people as a whole a lasting, perpetual covenant, one that can be identified with his acts of commitment to David. The implications are spelled out in a comparison with David's position and role. In his heyday David had been in the position of leader and commander in relation to surrounding peoples, and had thus been a witness to Yahweh's acts. Now Jacob-Israel is going to call a nation it does not acknowledge, and a nation that has not acknowledged it is going to run to it—"for the sake of Yahweh your God, of the Holy One of Israel, because he is glorifying you." The act of transformation that Yahweh is bringing about will enable the people as a whole to fulfill the role that David once fulfilled. There had once been a special covenant relationship between Yahweh and David as his servant, through which Yahweh had worked in the world and won some acknowledgment in the world. Now Yahweh will make such a covenant relationship with the people as a whole (in keeping with the original covenant relationship, before Israel dreamed up the idea of having a king), and as his servant or servants and witnesses or witness Jacob-Israel will see the world acknowledging Yahweh because of what he does with it.

The challenge to Jacob-Israel is to turn to Yahweh and be willing to submit to his intention regarding the fulfillment of his purpose, rather than continuing to insist on working with its own ideas about how that should work out (Is 55:6-13).

5

Isaiah 56–66

Whereas Isaiah 40–55 is the most linear of the collages, Isaiah 56–66 forms the neatest chiasm. It works as follows:

Preface and postscript: the place of foreigners in the service of Yahweh 56:1-8 ⟺ 66:18-24
Yahweh's challenges concerning the Jerusalem community's life 56:9–59:8 ⟺ 65:1–66:17
Prayers for Yahweh's forgiveness and restoration 59:9-15a ⟺ 63:7–64:12 [11]
Visions of Yahweh acting in judgment 59:15b-21 ⟺ 63:1-6
Visions of Jerusalem restored 60:1-22 ⟺ 61:10–62:12
The prophet's commission 61:1-9

Figure 5.1

Whereas a linear arrangement suggests that things are going somewhere, a chiasm suggests that they are simply going around and around. Such is the dominant impression conveyed by the final collage. No doubt Yahweh is going to fulfill his purpose, but at the moment the community is marking time.

The promise and the challenge of this situation are expressed in the opening lines of the collage:

> Guard the exercise of judgment, act in faithfulness,
> Because my deliverance is near to coming, my faithfulness to manifesting.
> (Is 56:1)

Rolf Rendtorff has noted how these opening lines constitute a summary of Isaiah 1–39 and 40–55.[1] Isaiah 1–39 has urged that Israel's life needs to be characterized by *mišpāṭ* and *ṣĕdāqâ*. Isaiah 40–55 has promised that Yahweh's action toward Israel is to be characterized by *mišpāṭ* and *ṣĕdāqâ*. But the reality that this collage will face and address is that neither of these desiderata has been fulfilled. The people still need to manifest *mišpāṭ* and *ṣĕdāqâ,* and also still need Yahweh to do so, and thus to effect the people's deliverance. In a way, therefore, the agenda for the final collage is the question of where we go from here, and the answer is that there is nowhere else to go.

An associated question concerns the relationship between the imperative and the statement in these opening lines of Isaiah 56. It is important that they do not make their relationship clear, because doing so would be bound to involve falling into heresy. On one hand, it is not the case that the community must make it possible for Yahweh to bring about their deliverance by their exercise of *mišpāṭ* and *ṣĕdāqâ*. That suggestion would imply that the fulfillment of Yahweh's purpose is ultimately dependent on human action, the heresy Paul seeks to safeguard against. But neither is it the case that Yahweh's purpose will be fulfilled irrespective of any human commitment to *mišpāṭ* and *ṣĕdāqâ,* the heresy James seeks to safeguard against. The point may be reexpressed by taking up the question of whether Yahweh's action is conditional on Israel's action, or whether his promise is unconditional. In fact, the conditional/unconditional model does not help an understanding of the dynamic of God's relationship with his people. In effect Paul makes this point in Romans 6, where he implies that a hypothetical person who asks whether we should sin in order that God's grace may abound has misunderstood Paul's entire argument; the object of God's gracious action was to bring into being a people characterized by *mišpāṭ* and *ṣĕdāqâ*. To put it another way, my relationship with my wife depends

---

[1]Rolf Rendtorff, *Canon and Theology* (Minneapolis: Fortress, 1993), pp. 181-89.

on the fact that we are committed to each other, but it would skew an understanding of the nature of the marriage relationship if we were to say that my commitment is conditional on Kathleen's. The matter is rather a question of definition. Marriage means mutual commitment. So does our relationship with God.

A Prophet as Yahweh's Anointed

If we consider the chapters' theological implications by starting from the center and moving outward, then with some logic we begin with the prophet's account of his commission (Is 61:1-9). He does not call himself Yahweh's servant; that expression comes in these chapters only in the plural, as a description of the people as a whole or of those within the people who are really committed to Yahweh. He does describe himself as one upon whom Yahweh's spirit has come (the expression that occurred in Is 42:1) and as one Yahweh has anointed (like Cyrus in Is 45:1 and like Yahweh's servant in Is 52:14), and he has a commission like that of Yahweh's servant in that his task is to bring good news to the lowly and freedom to prisoners. As happens in Isaiah 40–55 he brings good news to Zion about rebuilding and restoration and about the nations coming to acknowledge what Yahweh has done for them. Most of his account of his commission thus takes up the imagery and promises of Isaiah 40–55; his task is to reaffirm those promises. The implication is that they have not yet been fulfilled.

The most striking, novel element in his commission is his declaration of "release" for captives, where he uses the word associated with the freeing of bondservants after their maximum of six years of service (see Jer 34) or the freeing of people to return to their own land where they have had to forfeit it, after a maximum of forty-nine years (see Lev 25). The implication is that the whole community is in a position like that of bondservants or of people who have had to forfeit their land, but that the years of service or forfeiture are about to come to an end. It will thus be the year of Yahweh's favor, the day of God's redress. These are two sides of the same coin. Yahweh will take redress upon Israel's overlords and show favor to his people by freeing them. The same implication emerges from

Jesus' taking this testimony onto his own lips as a description of his vocation, though he separates favor and redress. First, in Luke 4:16-19 he stops his quotation from Isaiah 61 after the reference to the year of Yahweh's favor. But then in Luke 21:22 in his prophecy about the destruction of the temple and the approach of the end, he speaks of the siege of Jerusalem as the days of redress and of the fulfillment of all that has been written. This second statement suggests a fulfillment of God's threats as well as God's promises.

On either side of his account of his commission are more systematic portraits of the restoration of Zion (Is 60:1-22; 61:10–62:12), which he announces as the subject of his message in that account of his commission. These portraits again reaffirm promises in Isaiah 40–55, but they express them in more glorious technicolor. The technicolor becomes even more dazzling when Yahweh speaks of creating a new heavens and a new earth (Is 65:17). He is not referring to a new physical cosmos; there is nothing wrong with the existent cosmos. He explains that he is referring to a new Jerusalem, which Isaiah 65:17-25 goes on to describe in pleasingly more down-to-earth terms than those in Isaiah 60–62. It will be a city where infant mortality and other forms of early death will disappear, and where people will be able to build houses and live in them and plant vineyards and eat their fruit (rather than having these taken over by others). People will live in an immediate relationship with Yahweh, and there will be harmonious relationships within nature.

THE NATIONS' DESTINY

Isaiah 60–62 opens with a promise that when darkness covers the nations but light dawns over Zion, the nations will be drawn to that light (Is 60:1-3). Yahweh goes on to address the city itself about their riches coming to it:

> Flocks of Qedar will gather to you;
> the rams of Nebaiot will minister to you.
> They will come up for acceptance on my altar,
> and I will glorify my glorious house. (Is 60:7)

In his account of his commission, after speaking of comfort for the people who mourn Zion (that is, the community as a whole grieving over its still-devastated state), the prophet declares that "they will rebuild the long-lasting ruins" (Is 61:4). In isolation it would be natural to infer that it is the people of Jerusalem themselves who do the rebuilding, but Isaiah 60 has already declared that foreigners will rebuild the city and serve it (Is 60:10). The nations will also bring the city's children back from across the seas (Is 60:9). It will be the foreigners who will look after flocks, fields and vineyards, while the Israelites function as Yahweh's priests (Is 61:5-6). One should not infer that either building or shepherding and farming are lowly or despised occupations. Most Israelites had always been happy undertaking these tasks, while the Levites looked after the work of the temple, and one can imagine that as many Levites would be glad to escape the mucky and laborious work of the temple as non-Levites would wish that they had the chance to be involved in it. Yet the picture of a transformation in Zion's fortunes does imply that there is a great reversal here. The children of the people who had humbled the city will bow down to acknowledge it as Yahweh's city, a transformation of fortune that will lead Zion to acknowledge Yahweh as its deliverer (Is 60:14-16).

There is thus some ambiguity about the implications for the nations of the work Yahweh intends to do in Zion according to Isaiah 60–62. On either side of these chapters that focus on transformation for Jerusalem are two short prophecies with more unequivocally negative implications for the nations (Is 59:15b-20; 63:1-6). The background is the fact that Judah is a people that cannot control its own destiny. It is ruled by a powerful empire. In the absence of there being any other entity to use in the way he had used Cyrus, Yahweh promises that he will personally intervene to deal with "the peoples" (Is 63:6; in this prophecy, Edom denotes not Yahweh's victim but simply the direction from which Yahweh comes, as in a passage such as Deut 33:2). As a result, people will "revere" Yahweh's name and Yahweh's splendor from west to east (Is 59:20). Is it a positive awe or a cowed fear?

The Position of Foreigners

As we continue to move outward from the center of the collage and of the chiasm to the outermost frame, the question of the position of individual foreigners surfaces. It was apparently tempting for "a foreigner . . . who has attached himself to Yahweh" to say "Yahweh will definitely separate me from among his people," as well as for a eunuch to suspect that he has no place in Israel because he cannot contribute to the future of the people (Is 56:3). Perhaps there was no foreigner thinking in these terms and the point is a theoretical one; the comment it introduces is designed to shape the community's attitudes. Yahweh intends not to be satisfied with merely gathering scattered Israel.

The prophet does not implicitly dispute the action of Ezra and Nehemiah in breaking up foreign marriages. He is speaking of foreigners who attach themselves to Yahweh—people who would later be called proselytes or converts. It is entirely possible to imagine that there would be people who took a tougher line on openness to foreigners than the one implied by Ezra and Nehemiah and who held a strictly ethnic view of who could count as Yahweh's people; the prophet disputes that view as firmly as he elsewhere disputes the idea that the community can properly embrace religious diversity. The community needs to comprise people who attach themselves to Yahweh.

The key indicator of doing so is a willingness to keep the sabbath (Is 56:2). That willingness is an expression of adherence to Yahweh's covenant. Again, we know from Nehemiah 10:31; 13:15-22 that the sabbath was under pressure in the period that may be the background to Isaiah 56–66 and that it could thus be a key marker of whether someone was obedient to Yahweh (compare also Is 58:13-14).

One might think that Isaiah 56:2-8 could hardly make more significant commitments about the relationship of foreigners to the community: they will minister to Yahweh, they will join in celebrations in the temple as a place of prayer, they will find acceptance for their burnt offerings and fellowship sacrifices on Yahweh's altar. Yet arguably Isaiah 66:18-24 does so; at least, it works out its implications in a more striking fashion. The passage begins with "nations and tongues" gathering and witnessing Yahweh's restoring of his people; it is thus speaking about the nations as entities, rather than about individuals in the manner of Isaiah 56:2-8. These representatives of the nations and tongues are apparently people who have "survived" crushing by the imperial powers, but such survivors will go off to testify to Yahweh's action for the benefit of nations that are further off (so perhaps the "missionaries" are nearer peoples such as Moab and Ammon). The response of nations further away to the arrival of this news will involve not only coming to worship Yahweh themselves but also facilitating the return of Judahites still scattered among them. Doing so will be like bringing an offering to Yahweh; and as the *coup de grâce,* the prophecy adds that Yahweh will take some of the foreigners as priests.

The collage as a whole can thus speak of Yahweh judging the nations, of the nations being drawn to the light in Jerusalem, of their enriching Zion, of their bringing Judahites back home, of their freeing Judahites to take on the role of directly serving Yahweh, of individual foreigners committing themselves to Yahweh, and of their having a share in the service of Yahweh. It's therefore possible to ask whether it is more "nationalistic" or more "universalist" (universalist not in the sense that everyone ends up in heaven but in the sense that God is concerned for all the nations in the world).

Yet that alternative doesn't get at the dynamic of the prophecy's attitude.

1. Like Isaiah 40–55 the prophecy is sometimes concerned with the nations as the superpower, the empire, the master whom Judah must serve and whom Yahweh intends to put down, and at other times concerned with the nations as a collection of peoples like Judah itself that are the superpower's underlings and that will benefit along with Judah from Yahweh's putting the superpower down.

2. Unlike Isaiah 40–55 it is sometimes concerned with the position of individual foreigners whom one can imagine being actual residents in Jerusalem, individuals like Rahab, Ruth and Uriah who are mentioned in connection with earlier times in Israel's story.

3. It is sometimes concerned with the fact that Judah's insecurity or pressure stems not only from the overlordship of the superpower but also

from the adversarial attitude of neighbors such as Ammon, Moab and Edom; but it can thus take a different stance toward these nations from the one it takes to peoples further away that do not impact it in this way.

4. Even its references to good things that Yahweh will do for the nations (such as giving them a role in the leading of worship) feature because of their positive significance for Judah itself. Their point is to enhance the dimensions of Yahweh's intentions in order to build up the morale and faith of the Judahite community. Thus the prophecy can be "universalist" (concerned for the nations) in part for "nationalist" reasons—that is, its talk of Yahweh's drawing the nations to Jerusalem enhances the wonder of what Yahweh will do for Judah.

5. Prophecies about the nations share a feature with prophecies about Judah, that they always presuppose that what happens, and what Yahweh does by way of bringing blessing or trouble, depends on the way people respond to the challenges put in front of them. The story of Jonah is the classic exposition of the way the fulfillment of Yahweh's declarations of judgment on a city or a nation is dependent on whether they turn from their oppressiveness and arrogance.

Prayer

Judah never saw anything as spectacular or final as what these prophecies promise about Yahweh's acting against the nations or acting to glorify Jerusalem. This fact did not stop Judah holding on to the promises; indeed, it likely encouraged the community in doing so. Judah sat in a position with which the Christian church can identify, because we have been waiting for two millennia for the fulfillment of promises about Jesus' appearing, yet we have not assumed that the promises were false. We are able to wait, because we have grounds for trusting the one who made the promises, and because we see recurrent partial fulfillments of them.

"In its time I will speed it," Yahweh says (Is 60:22). It is a subtle declaration, both of whose parts are important. On one hand, the action will come only "in its time," not in accordance with a schedule that prophet or audience can determine. As the New Testament puts it, a day or a millennium are the same thing to God (2 Pet 3:8). On the other hand, "I will speed it." People are not to feel discouraged or to lose hope, and neither are they to expect that the fulfillment will take *too* long. Yahweh will indeed act.

Making promises exposes Yahweh to prayer pressure, which is applied by two further sections of the prophecy, working from the center outward (Is 59:9-15a; 63:7–64:12 [11]). Both prayers acknowledge the waywardness of the community but do not assume that this waywardness makes it impossible to urge Yahweh to take action on the community's behalf. Perhaps such prayer makes the assumption about God that we have noted already, that Yahweh has bound himself in commitment to Israel, so that it can appeal for Yahweh to act in faithfulness and in the exercise of authority on its behalf even though it does so as a wayward people. This possibility would link with the way the prophet by virtue of his position occupies a place that involves identifying with both Yahweh and the people. Identified with Yahweh, he has to own the community's waywardness. Identified with the community, he also has to voice its prayer—or rather voice the kind of prayer it needs to pray.

The second, much longer prayer indeed sums up something of the nature of the relationship between Yahweh and the people as it has obtained through the book called Isaiah. The book more or less began with Yahweh's sense of offense at the way his children have related to him as their father (Is 1:2), and here it almost ends with a parallel awareness. Yahweh had looked for a responsiveness on the part of these children; the children themselves now recall how Yahweh had carried their ancestors like a father, and they look for more of a fatherly attitude on Yahweh's part (Is 63:8, 9, 16; 64:9 [8]). Isaiah 34–35 and 40–55, and the promises in Isaiah 59:15b–63:6, have used another family metaphor in speaking of Yahweh as restorer (*gō'ēl*); this prayer begins from the way Yahweh acted as restorer at the beginning and wants to know why there is no such action now (Is 63:9, 16).

The prayer thus matches the Psalms in the confrontational nature of its protest. It not only acknowledges that the people have been wayward but also blames Yahweh for that fact: "Why, Yahweh, do you make us wander from your ways, make our mind become hard so that we don't revere you?"

(Is 63:17). It urges Yahweh to "turn," the verb commonly translated "repent" (Is 63:17), and it accuses Yahweh of "afflicting" Israel, the word once used of the Egyptians' treatment of Israel in Egypt (Is 64:12 [11]). It implies that Yahweh's neglect and punishment are surely excessive.

A remarkable aspect of the relationship between Yahweh and Israel as Isaiah and the Psalms describe it is that it has the kind of depth and strength in which no holds need to be barred. Israel can speak straight to Yahweh and Yahweh can speak straight back, without this confrontation imperiling the reality of the relationship. So Yahweh responds to this prayer by blowing a fuse and expostulating about its outrageous nature (Is 65:1-2). As if this community could claim it has been calling on Yahweh for years when the calling has been in the other direction! The motif of call and response then recurs in the book's last two chapters (Is 65:12, 24; 66:5).

TRUE RELIGION

The major sections outside the two prayers focus on the nature of true religion. It has two main aspects. True worship needs to be offered to Yahweh alone and offered in a way that recognizes who Yahweh truly is. The reason for Yahweh's snorting response to the people's prayer is that this prayer is accompanied by abhorrent religious practices (Is 65:1-12). People take part in worship that involves seeking the help of gods other than Yahweh, and they are even prepared to sacrifice children in the course of doing so (Is 57:3-13). Quite likely they saw themselves as still committed to Yahweh; they would see the other deities as Yahweh's underlings or agents, and they would see their sacrifices as offered to Yahweh indirectly if not directly. But they have continued the assimilation to the traditional religion of Canaan that commonly characterized Israel. They need, therefore, to turn back to Yahweh as the one who dwells "on high and holy" but also "with the crushed and low in spirit" (Is 57:15).

The other aspect of true religion is that it needs to be accompanied by right living outside worship, but alongside apostate faith is social breakdown. The prophecy's critique grievously parallels the critique from two centuries ago—in other words, the last part of Isaiah corresponds to the first. We have come full circle. People with power in the community focus on doing well for themselves and on indulging themselves, and they ignore (or encourage) the way faithful people become the victims of oppression and lose their lives one way or another (Is 56:9–57:2).

Indeed, it is possible to be faithful in living by Yahweh's religious expectations yet to discover that this kind of faithfulness does not count. Once more the prophecy parallels the critique near the opening of Isaiah, which condemned heartfelt, sacrificial, prayerful worship that was unaccompanied by *mišpāṭ* and *ṣĕdāqâ* (Is 1:10-20). In Isaiah 58, people are committed to fasting, which can have a number of significances. One is that fasting can back up prayer, but people are finding that it does not work, and the reason is that at the same time as fasting they are involved in the exploitation and ill treatment of their employees. There is thus a further parallel with Isaiah 1, in that the prophecy is not suggesting that there is a mismatch between people's outward practice and their inner attitude; they are quite sincere in their seeking God. The problem lies in the mismatch between two aspects of their outward lives. They are looking for Yahweh to act with *mišpāṭ* and *ṣĕdāqâ,* but they are not acting in that way themselves (Is 58:2). In a further parallel with the earlier polemic, the prophecy is not concerned with the theoretical question of whether a particular form of religion is proper or necessary, but with a practical question about this particular community's fasting. Raising the question issues in the prophecy's turning fasting into a metaphor for a different form of self-denial and self-giving (Is 58:6-12), action that *is* an expression of *mišpāṭ* and *ṣĕdāqâ.* It would have been easy for the prophecy to make a parallel point about the sabbath as designed to give one's employees a day off. Instead it emphasizes the other aspect of the fasting polemic. The key question for people is whether they have chance to do what they want in their business affairs, and thereby to ignore Yahweh's claim on time (Is 58:13-14).

True religion doesn't really need a temple (Is 66:1-2). The enthusiasm for temple worship elsewhere in this collage and elsewhere in Isaiah suggests that in principle Isaiah 66 is not in opposition to the temple. One might compare the comments on the temple with the comments on fasting, since the comments on the temple lead into further critique of people who can combine proper sacrificial offerings with improper ones (Is 66:3). Like the comments on fasting and the earlier comments on worship, then, the prophecy is more concerned with the place of the temple in this people's thinking and life than with the theoretical question of whether temples are a good thing. But one might also compare the dual attitude that the book called Isaiah takes to Davidic kingship, which it both affirms (e.g., Is 37:35) and reinterprets (Is 55:3-5). Its dual attitude to monarchy and temple corresponds to the Old Testament's own dual attitude to both of these institutions. Both of them are human ideas about which Yahweh is uneasy but which he is prepared to go with.

Who Are Yahweh's Servants?

Near the end of Isaiah 40–55 a strange thing happens: following on many occurrences of the expression "Yahweh's servant" (or "my/his servant") there suddenly occurs the plural "Yahweh's servants" as a designation of people to whom Yahweh will allocate the position whose description then follows (Is 54:17). Who are these servants?

On the next two occurrences of the term, in Isaiah 56:6; 63:17, it designates the members of Israel as a group, but in Isaiah 65:13-15; 66:14 it refers to the faithful *within* Israel, the real servants of Yahweh within Israel as a whole. In between these two pairs of passages, in Isaiah 65:8-9 one could understand the plural either way. There is a certain appropriateness in that ambiguity, as it reflects the fact that ideally the entire people comprises Yahweh's servants, even though in practice only part of the people behaves in a way that makes that designation apposite. In Isaiah 40–55 "Yahweh's servant" denoted the people as a whole or the prophet as an individual, but never a faithful group within Israel. Here with some appropriateness the expression "Yahweh's servants" can be used with reference to the people who are faithful. They are also "my chosen ones" (Is 65:15), another term that by its nature refers to the community as a whole but is now given this narrower reference.

Yahweh's servants are not only the subgroup that is faithful; they are also people who are repudiated and excluded (Is 66:5). It seems, then, that the nonfaithful are the people with power in connection with the worship of the temple and/or the life of the city. But their abandonment of faithfulness, their turning away from true religion, has turned them into Yahweh's foes, and they will pay the price that would otherwise be exacted only from oppressive foreign nations.

The book called Isaiah almost ends by declaring that "new moon by new moon, sabbath by sabbath, all flesh will come to bow low before me" (Is 66:23). Yet it actually ends with a further declaration: "People will go out and look at the corpses of the individuals who rebelled against me, because their worm will not die and their fire will not go out; it will be a horror to all flesh" (Is 66:24). The close of the book thereby places a decision before its readers. Will you be like the people who bow low before Yahweh? Or the people whose bodies are thrown onto a pile for decaying or burning?

PART TWO

The THEOLOGY *That* EMERGES *from* ISAIAH

At some time in the Persian period or possibly the Greek period (sometime between 500 and 200 B.C.) the process whereby the book called Isaiah developed came to an end, and the book as we have it came into existence. What theology emerges from this book as a whole?

6

Revelation

Words from Yahweh Mediated Through Human Agents

The ***book called Isaiah begins*** with the heading, "The vision (*ḥāzôn*) of Isaiah ben Amoz, which he saw concerning Judah and Jerusalem in the time of Uzziah, Jotham, Ahaz, and Hezekiah, kings of Judah" (Is 1:1). The heading refers directly to the chapter that follows, but Isaiah 1 itself does introduce the book as a whole, and its own heading has implications in connection with the book as a whole.

What we read in Isaiah 1 is a vision, something the prophet saw that not everyone could see. The heavens opened and he saw visions of God. More literally or more usually, to judge from this chapter, he heard God speak (Is 1:2, 10, 11, 18, 20, 24). Slightly paradoxically, the chapter's colophon similarly describes it as "the word that Isaiah ben Amoz saw (*ḥāzâ*) concerning Judah and Jerusalem." What we read in Isaiah 1, and more broadly in the book that this chapter introduces, is not something that the prophet thought up in the way I am thinking up this chapter, but something that presented itself to him. He did not devise the words; they came to him. He overheard Yahweh speaking, perhaps externalizing an inner reflection or making a declaration to the court in the heavens ("Children I reared, brought up, and they—they rebelled against me!" [Is 1:2]).

Subsequently, Isaiah speaks like a messenger who repeats the words of his master, "the Lord Yahweh has said this" (e.g., Is 7:7; 10:24). There is a solemnity about being addressed by someone who comes with the Great King's authority and speaks with the "I" of the great king, as if he *were* the great king (cf. Is 36:4, 14, 16). That is how a prophet speaks as Yahweh's messenger, as if he *were* the Great King. He brings the great king's presence; he speaks performatively. The opening chapter uses the less common *yiqtol* formulation "Yahweh says" (Is 1:11, 18), which in its way might be more worrying. Yahweh did not merely say this once. It is a statement Yahweh continues to aver. The matter's seriousness is underlined by other formulations the prophet uses. He speaks "the word of Yahweh" (Is 1:10). His message is something that "the mouth of Yahweh spoke" (Is 1:20). The prophet transmits "the declaration (*nĕ'um*) of the Lord Yahweh Armies" (Is 1:24). The book's opening thus suggests a revelation with the authenticity and demand of divine dictation. "Yahweh Armies revealed himself in my ears" (Is 22:14). Sometimes one indeed has the impression that the prophet transmits words that he has heard Yahweh speak, like a stenographer who records the words spoken in court.

Yet the book begins by describing what follows not as "the vision of Yahweh" but as "the vision of Isaiah ben Amoz." A particular person here reports what he sees and hears. Different people may all give absolutely accurate accounts of a scene they have witnessed, but their accounts may all be different, and they will reflect their angle of vision. To the scene opening up before him, Isaiah ben Amoz brings an angle of vision that differs from the one Jeremiah or Ezekiel would bring to it. Revelation comes via the human person.

When an envoy relates Sennacherib's message to Hezekiah, he may sometimes pass on his king's actual words, but he also engages in dialogue with Hezekiah's staff and continues then to speak as if relating the king's own words. He has the authority to speak on his king's behalf in the way that seems appropriate in the context. Even when he himself devises the words, he can use the "I" of his king. His words have his king's authority. They are the king's words, even though he formulates them. Something similar is true of Isaiah ben Amoz. Some of what he says represents what he overheard in the divine council. Some represents what he formulated in light of what he has heard Yahweh say. It is all his "vision," and it all reflects his angle of vision, but it all has Yahweh's authority.

Further, while the prophet's human voice is the means through which Yahweh's words are uttered, the prophet's human person brings a revelation of Yahweh in a broader sense. Implicitly his name, "Yahweh-is-deliverance," does so; it embodies his message. His children's names also do it (Is 7:3 with Is 10:21-22; 8:1-4; perhaps also Is 7:14). He and his children are signs and portents in Israel from Yahweh (Is 8:18). Isaiah ben Amoz represents his message even more concretely when he walks around the city as Yahweh's servant stripped of his clothes as a sign and portent of the coming fate of Egypt and Sudan, whose alliance Judah would therefore be unwise to rely on (Is 20:1-6). And in return, as the prophet who represents Yahweh, he gets treated in the same way as people treat Yahweh (Is 28:7-10).

If being a prophet means being identified with Yahweh in the passage just noted, in Isaiah 40–55 it means being identified with Israel. When Yahweh gives the bidding "Preach," the prophet replies, "Preach what?" Israel is withered by the hot, divine breath of Yahweh's wrath; how can it listen to preaching? The analysis is correct, but the prophet has forgotten one factor: "our God's word stands forever" (Is 40:8). When Yahweh says something, such as the words in Isaiah 40:1-5, they have their effect, like the word Yahweh sent on Ephraim so that it caused terrible destruction (Is 9:8-9 [7-8]), but now that effect is more positive. So the fact that "Sovereign Yahweh has sent me with his breath" (Is 48:16b) means that the prophet's words will find fulfillment.

In Isaiah 49:1-6 the prophet gives the first episode of testimony to the way Yahweh is working out the implications of that identification with Israel. This identification is with Israel as the means of fulfilling a ministry on Yahweh's behalf. We have learned from Isaiah 41–48 that Israel is supposed to be Yahweh's servant but is incapable of fulfilling that role. But Isaiah ben Amoz had already functioned as Yahweh's servant (Is 20:3), and Yahweh has now issued the same commission to the prophet who speaks in Isaiah 49:1-6. "Yahweh summoned me from the womb . . . and said to me,

'You are my servant, Israel in whom I will display my attractiveness.'" The prophet is to embody the service of Yahweh that Israel is called to and is still destined for, and thus "to turn Jacob back to him, to stop Israel withdrawing." The trouble is that this is a tough task, perhaps both because of the community's resistance and because of Babylonian opposition. Ironically, the prophet thus comes again to resemble Israel in reckoning that everything is pointless (Is 49:4a; cf. Is 40:6-7, 27). But a person who is tempted to that view has to argue with his or her self and refuse to settle for that conclusion (Is 49:4b). And further, Yahweh points out that being the means of restoring Israel will also imply being a means of Yahweh's light and deliverance reaching the rest of the world (Is 49:5-6).

There is more to the toughness of the task. Being Yahweh's servant means listening to Yahweh in the manner of a disciple and doing what the master says, but that listening and responsiveness brings shame and persecution (Is 50:4-6). Fortunately there is also more to the toughness of the prophet (Is 50:7-9).

Indeed, there is much more to the toughness of the task, and to the identification with the community. In the vision presupposed by Isaiah 52:13–53:12, the prophet is on the way to death (it is impossible to know whether this is where things are in "real time"). The community initially assumes that this fact confirms its convictions about the prophet, but it is eventually won over to the realization that actually this servant of Yahweh suffers for the sake of a ministry to them. This fact then leads to the servant's turning the undeserved suffering that this ministry entails into an offering to Yahweh, in the hope that this huge act of obedience might counterbalance, counteract or compensate for the community's own willfulness. Not only is Yahweh behind his doing so, but also Yahweh's own promise is that this suffering will not be the end. The self-offering will be effective. Horrific affliction will be succeeded by a spectacular anointing. And the prophet will be the means whereby cleansing comes to nations and kings.

Regarding the prophet who speaks in Isaiah 59:21, Yahweh subsequently promises the faithful that "my spirit which is on you and my words which I have put in your mouth will not be absent from your mouth"; nor will they be absent from the mouths of his descendants. A first fulfillment of that promise comes in Isaiah 61:1. "The spirit of the Lord Yahweh is on me, because he has anointed me." Prophets were not usually anointed; anointing is the rite whereby a priest consecrates a king or priest. Here Yahweh is the one who anoints, and the declaration also takes up the promise in Isaiah 52:14.

He has sent me to bring news to the weak,
  to bind up the wounded in heart,
to proclaim release to captives,
  the opening of eyes to prisoners,
to proclaim a year of favor for Yahweh,
  a day of redress for our God,
to comfort all who mourn,
  to provide for the people who grieve in Zion—
to give them a garland instead of ashes,
  joyful oil instead of grief,
a praise garment instead
  of a fainting spirit. (Is 61:1-3)

In other words, this prophet continues the ministry exercised by the prophet who speaks in Isaiah 40–55, as the community still experiences weakness, hurt, servitude and abandonment by Yahweh. The prophet's task is thus to urge Yahweh to act in faithfulness and deliverance and also to commission other people to keep reminding Yahweh of his commitment to establish and glorify Jerusalem (Is 62:1-7).

There is another facet of Isaiah that relates to traditional discussion of revelation and its relationship to Scripture. Isaiah 1–39 and 40–55 incorporate material explicitly addressing the eighth century and the 540s. Isaiah 56–66 incorporates material implicitly addressing a subsequent context, perhaps the latter part of the sixth century, and the book may also include other material that implicitly addresses other contexts, such as the Josianic period or the fifth or fourth century. Yet Isaiah is not simply an anthology of messages from Yahweh given via different prophets but one in which a message in one of the collages sometimes becomes the text on which a later message is based, the text for a subsequent sermon. In other words, earlier material within the book (and for that matter, words that appear in other prophetic books such as Jeremiah) have become the recognized word of God on which later material preaches. One example is the way Isaiah 2:2-4 is taken up and nuanced in Isaiah 42:1-4.[1] Another example is the way motifs recur in the book, such as blindness (Is 6:9-10; 29:9-10; 32:3; 35:5; 42:7; 43:8) or potter and clay (Is 29:16; 45:9; 64:8 [7]) or the preparing of Yahweh's way (Is 40:3; 57:14). The manner in which the sermon takes up the text varies. In the first case it nuances it; in the second it says "Yes, but/and now. . . ." In the third it riffs on it; in the fourth, it reapplies it. In each case it assumes that ongoing significance attaches to earlier words of Yahweh. The revelation to the prophet and through the prophet has become a text that can be illuminating for subsequent generations, and it invites them to reflect on what Yahweh is doing with them in light of it.

When theologians used to begin their systematic work with a consideration of revelation, this ordering reflected more the issues of the Enlightenment era than the logic of Scripture as a whole. Nevertheless this ordering does correspond to the way Isaiah and other prophetic books begin. What we read in the book are words from Yahweh mediated through human agents.

[1]In this case as in others, the second passage may actually be earlier than the first, in which case the flow from text to exposition is the reverse, but this does not affect the principle; the framework of intertextuality helps here.

7

The God of Israel, the Holy One, Yahweh Armies

In considering the substance of Isaianic theology, the obvious starting point is the book's characteristic description of Yahweh as "Israel's Holy One," which occurs in all three main parts of the book (e.g., Is 1:4; 17:7; 29:19; 37:23; 41:14; 55:5; 60:9). Further, whereas it occurs thirty times in the Old Testament as a whole, twenty-five of these are in Isaiah (three come in the Psalms, two in Jeremiah). So it is distinctively characteristic of the book. Perhaps Isaiah ben Amoz devised it, or perhaps he adopted an expression already in occasional use. In either case, the experience described in Isaiah 6:1-13 may lie behind his use of the title. In that chapter he relates a vision of Yahweh in the palace in the heavens and of seraphs proclaiming, "Holy, holy, holy, Yahweh Armies, his splendor is the filling of the whole earth." The seraphs' reticence, covering their faces, the shaking of the doorframe, the smoke filling the house, all combine to underline the scene's awe, and thus the significance of the declaration that Yahweh is not merely once holy, or twice holy, but thrice holy; not merely holy, or very holy, but utterly holy. These accompaniments and reactions also point to the significance of the notion of holiness. In itself it is not a moral category but a metaphysical one. To be holy is to belong to a different realm from the everyday, the worldly, the human, the created, the this-worldly. It is to belong to the heavenly realm, the supernatural world. By definition, beings such as gods and angels are holy, whether or not they are very moral. To say that Yahweh is thrice-holy is to say that Yahweh is the ultimate in the supernatural, extraordinary, uncreated, heavenly. In reporting the threefold cry, Isaiah is not referring to God's own threefold nature, but one can see how the cry would be open to being appropriated and built on when the idea of God being Father, Son and Holy Spirit was articulated.

The point about God's absolute sovereignty is underlined by the epithet "Yahweh Armies," *Yahweh ṣĕbā'ôt.* This title is also characteristic of Isaiah 1–55 (e.g., Is 1:9; 13:4; 24:23; 28:5; 37:16; 44:6; 54:5), though it goes back at least to Yahweh's "palace" at Shiloh, where it is associated with the covenant chest (1 Sam 1:3, 11; 4:4). From there it perhaps found its way to Yahweh's "palace" at Jerusalem, where Isaiah would have been familiar with it (as perhaps with "Israel's Holy One"). The expression itself is somewhat enigmatic, as LXX's transliteration *sabaōth* in Isaiah reflects, though its general point is clear. In the Psalms, LXX renders "Lord of the powers," though it is debatable whether grammatically the name Yahweh can thus be construed as construct. Elsewhere LXX renders *pantokratōr,* "all-mighty." Either translation conveys the likely sense, if less vividly than the Hebrew, which points to Yahweh's power as warrior. Yahweh controls or embodies all forceful might, all strength and power. That underscores the impression of the extraordinary and supernatural conveyed by the epithet "thrice holy." Yahweh Armies musters an army for war (Is 13:4). "Yahweh Armies will attend on high to the army on high, and on the earth to the kings of the earth" (Is 24:21). "Yahweh Armies will come down to make war on Mount Zion and its hill" (Is 31:4). Yahweh is a God of war, raging and shouting like a warrior, shrieking like a birthing woman (Is 42:13-14). While the title "Yahweh Armies" does not occur in Isaiah 56–66, these chapters incorporate two further powerful expositions of the image of Yahweh the warrior. He puts on armor to give his foes their deserts (Is 59:15b-19); he comes from the east looking like a viticulturist covered in grape juice, but the grape juice stands for blood (Is 63:1-6). Further, Yahweh is one who made war against Israel (Is 63:10).

So warfare is not left to earthly powers. Sennacherib thinks that he is the only military power in the Middle East. And Hezekiah knows that "the kings of Assyria have wasted all the lands (and their land) and set their gods on fire (because they were not gods but the work of human hands, wood and stone) and done away with them." He therefore bids Yahweh to act "so that all earth's kingdoms may acknowledge that you alone are Yahweh" (Is 37:18-20).

This might seem not a very profound acknowledgment, but it involves an ellipse that recurs in succeeding chapters. To say that Yahweh is the ultimate supernatural, extraordinary, uncreated, sovereign, heavenly being is in effect to say that Yahweh is the only God. We have noted in connection with Isaiah 40–55 that it is misleading to say that this amounts to an assertion of monotheism; it is a bigger declaration than that one. Isaiah does not start from the question of how many gods there are or whether there is a principle of unity behind reality but from the question of who is God and from the unrivaled holiness of Yahweh. There is such a difference between Yahweh and other gods that only Yahweh deserves the description "God." The terms *Yahweh* and *God* have different meaning but the same reference; there is only one person to whom either term applies.

So to "acknowledge that you alone are Yahweh" is to acknowledge that Yahweh alone is God. That Yahweh alone is God is evidenced by the story of Yahweh's activity over the centuries, embodied in Abraham and Cyrus, and by the associated record of Yahweh's speaking over the centuries about the events that were to take place then and are taking place now (Is 41:1-7, 21-29; 43:9-13). "I am first and I am last; apart from me there is no God" (Is 44:6). "I am the one, I am first, yes, I am last" (Is 48:12). As the first, Yahweh is the creator; as the last, Yahweh is able to declare an intention in history and fulfill it, and has done so, and has thus provided the evidence of being such a God (Is 44:6-8; 48:12-16a). It is as the creator that Yahweh controls the army in the heavens, and as the creator that Yahweh is greater than the nations that seem to be in control of Israel's destiny, than the images that the nations construct, than the kings who are so much more impressive than Judah's, and than that heavenly army itself (Is 40:12-26). There are times when Yahweh has hidden and neither spoken nor acted, but such withdrawal is a reaction to Israel's rebellion. It is not Yahweh's characteristic stance (Is 45:14-19; 48:3-8, 16).

I am Yahweh and there is no other,
shaper of light and creator of dark,
Maker of well-being and creator of adversity,
I am Yahweh, maker of all these. (Is 45:6-7)

Yahweh brings about the good things and the bad things that happen, the flourishing of Israel and its calamities, the victories and the defeats. No one else is involved.

Yahweh therefore contrasts with the images that Israelites and other peoples often take seriously. The very process of their manufacture shows that they are stupid, or rather that people who take them seriously are stupid (Is 44:9-20). They obviously cannot do anything. In theory, of course, people did not identify images with the gods they represent, but in practice, people do so. And anyway, paradoxically, the images represent the gods very well. The images can neither speak nor act; neither can the gods. Isaiah 46 imagines the great Babylonian gods bowing down to be carried into captivity; their needing to be carried contrasts with Yahweh's being the God who carries people (Is 46:1-4). People cry out to the images, and they do not answer; they cannot save from distress (Is 46:7).

Further, the fact that Yahweh alone is God is reason why Israel has no business having recourse to any traditional supernatural and spiritual resources, as the book emphasizes at its opening and closing (Is 1:29-31; 65:1-12).

8

Holy as Upright and Merciful

For Yahweh to be the thrice holy, the all-mighty God, can constitute good news or bad news. Both implications are worked out in Isaiah, in a way that gives moral content to the metaphysical epithet *holy.*

Isaiah ben Amoz sees the powerful people in Judah as characterized by self-indulgence, confidence that they will be able to maintain their position and refusal to think about what Yahweh may be intending (Is 5:8-14). But in his vision,

> Humanity has bowed itself down, people have become low,
> the eyes of the majestic have become low.
> But Yahweh Armies has become majestic in exercising authority,
> as the holy God has made himself holy in doing right. (Is 5:15-16)

In this vision, the people with power and prestige in society are now the lowly. It has come about because Yahweh has acted and demonstrated where real power lies. The powerful are the people who should have been exercising authority in the right way, exercising *mišpāṭ* and *ṣědāqâ* (cf. Is 56:1). But instead of *mišpāṭ* and *ṣědāqâ,* Yahweh found *miśpāḥ* and *ṣěʿāqâ,* "pouring [of blood] and crying out" (Is 5:7). Yahweh has now therefore intervened to exercise *mišpāṭ* and *ṣědāqâ* against them and for the ordinary people. And it is in this way that Yahweh has "made himself holy" or manifested holiness (*qādaš* niphal). Holiness manifests itself in *mišpāṭ* and *ṣědāqâ.* There is thus a positive aspect to this manifestation of holiness; it means taking action on behalf of people who are abused. But Isaiah here focuses on its negative aspect (the New Jewish Publication Society translation [NJPS] has "proved holy by retribution"), which is necessary if the positive is to be achieved.

Yahweh thus also manifests majesty. Isaiah 2 especially stresses the contrast between human majesty and divine majesty, and Isaiah 3:18–4:1 adds its application to the women of standing in the community (compare Is 32:9-14 following on Is 32:1-8). Yahweh's action means that the people who look majestic have their majesty exposed as tawdry (Is 28:1-4). Isaiah emphasizes the great anger Yahweh can generate in this connection. The phrase "for all this, his anger has not turned; his hand is still extended" recurs (e.g., Is 5:25), suggesting how vast is the reservoir of Yahweh's anger at people's misuse of their intelligence and their power, their self-assertiveness and their self-indulgence.

In itself, Yahweh's holiness and majesty appropriately inspire both trust and confidence and also respect and awe (Is 7:1-17; 8:1-13). The trouble is that the nation offers Yahweh neither. Metaphorically speaking, Jerusalem is sexually immoral (Is 1:21); it betrays its relationship with Yahweh by having recourse to other political and religious resources (Is 2:6-22; 8:19-22). Shrewd people in the society have appropriated a disproportionate amount of the community's resources. All this waywardness would make people shrink back from the majestic and holy God; Yahweh's holiness and majesty suggest the taking of action against them. The connotations of majestic holiness are threatening. But for the people who have no power and are denied resources, Yahweh's majestic holiness is an encouragement.

The encouraging implications of Yahweh's holiness become explicit in a surprising way in Isaiah 40–55. Here, "Israel's Holy One is your restorer" (Is 41:14; cf. Is 43:3; 47:4; 48:17; 49:7; 54:5), "your deliverer" (Is 43:3). As its restorer (*gō'ēl*), Yahweh behaves like the member of an extended family who has the resources to come to the aid of another family member in trouble—for instance by helping them avoid or escape debt servitude and/or by taking action against people who have wronged them. A restorer is thus a deliverer. In a sense, then, describing Yahweh as restorer only provides a fresh image for the action described in Isaiah 5. But there the focus lay on the negative aspect to the restorer's action. The addressees were the abusers. Here the focus lies on the positive aspect to the action, and the addressees are the victims. It is, however, a problem that they are essentially the same people, or at least their descendants, who have the same moral profile as they had before. Whether the prophet is addressing people in exile or left behind in Jerusalem, they are a people that had turned its back on Yahweh in a number of ways. And the chapters make clear that nothing has changed. So it would be quite reasonable for Yahweh to continue to "make himself holy in doing right" by leaving them to their own devices. Instead, the Holy One is acting as their restorer, relating to this mob of rebels on the basis of their being part of the Holy One's family.

In the Old Testament, the relationship between Yahweh and Israel can be described in covenantal terms. But the trouble with a covenant is that people enter into it voluntarily and can get out of it. Family relationships are different. People cannot choose whether to belong to their family. Family imposes obligations on us whether we like it or not; evading them brings terrible shame. Isaiah 40–55 mostly utilizes family imagery rather than covenant imagery. Jacob-Israel has no moral claim on Yahweh ("children I reared, brought up, and they—they rebelled against me!" [Is 1:2]), but Yahweh accepts family obligations to Jacob-Israel, acting like a prodigal father reaching out to his son before he even takes a step toward home.

And it is as the Holy One that Yahweh does so. It is Israel's Holy One who is its restorer. The Holy One is the creator of Israel (Is 43:15), its shaper (Is 45:11), the one who chose it (Is 49:7). So the relationship between Yahweh and Israel is a historical one (and thus a covenantal one) as well as a familial one. Yahweh brought Israel into being and chose Israel. Israel thus became Yahweh's people, and Yahweh became Israel's God. Yahweh became Israel's Holy One, establishing a relationship that was henceforth both historical and familial.

So Yahweh's being the Holy One is both solemn news (it can imply Yahweh acting against you) and encouraging news (it can imply Yahweh acting for you). If you do wrong, you should expect Yahweh to act against you, though there is no formula here; the fact that Yahweh is committed to you may mean you find Yahweh acting in mercy. Yahweh is the high and lofty one, the eternal and Holy One, who dwells on high; Yahweh also dwells with the crushed and humbled in spirit (Is 57:15-19), people who have been crushed and humbled by Yahweh because of their waywardness. Yahweh gets angry, confronts, withdraws and hits, but Yahweh does not stay angry—he heals, comforts and brings well-being. "The heavens are my throne and the earth is my footstool," so where could one build Yahweh a house (Is 66:1)? "But to this person I pay attention, to the weak and broken-spirited, to the person who trembles at my word" (Is 66:2). Yahweh dwells with them, reviving their hearts and spirits, even when they do not deserve it.

The use of *mišpāṭ* and *ṣĕdāqâ* in the same context as talk of restoration and deliverance makes the same point. The exercise of authority (*mišpāṭ*) was bad news in Isaiah 5:16. It is good news in Isaiah 40:27; 42:1, 3, 4; 49:4; 51:4; it means Yahweh is taking decisive action on Israel's behalf. Yahweh's doing the right thing (*ṣĕdāqâ*) was bad news in Isaiah 5:16; it is good news in Isaiah 45:8, 23, 24; 46:12, 13; 48:18; 51:6, 8; 54:17 (compare *ṣedeq* in Is 41:2, 10; 42:6, 21; 45:8, 13, 19; 51:1, 5, 7). Doing the right thing has relational implications; *ṣĕdāqâ* does not merely imply acting in light of a principle of justice, but doing the right thing in light of relationships in one's community. An implication is that there can be a tension for Yahweh as for parents or the elders in a community about whether one takes action against people who do wrong, or whether one holds back in mercy. Yahweh's letting Jerusalem fall was an act of *ṣĕdāqâ;* Yahweh's restoring Jerusalem is an act of *ṣĕdāqâ.* Once again, this restoration does not happen because Israel deserves it, so that the restoration would be an act of justice. Justice would mean leaving Judahites in exile and leaving the temple in ruins; *ṣĕdāqâ* means Yahweh's coming back to Jerusalem and bringing exiled Judahites home there.

Yet Isaiah remains aware that there is something odd about Yahweh acting violently against Judah. When Isaiah 28:21-22 speaks of Yahweh arising in a way that stands in continuity with events in the great days of David, this arising actually involves Judah being the victim, not the beneficiary, of Yahweh's action. It is thus a "strange" deed, an act that is "foreign" to Yahweh. It does not come naturally to act in judgment. Yahweh is capable of summoning up the resources to undertake this alien deed, so people had better listen and not scoff at the prospect. But it remains an alien deed. Faithfulness, mercy and protection are more natural to Yahweh than wrath and punishment. The long story of Israel is one that involves Yahweh acting in wrath, but much more often it involves Yahweh's holding back from doing so. After describing the way Yahweh acts in wrath, the way Lamentations makes the point is by noting that Yahweh does so only "unwillingly" (Lam 3:33)—more literally, when he afflicts people, it is "not from the heart," not from the center of who he is.

In origin, then, holiness is a metaphysical rather than a moral term; it denotes Yahweh as the supernatural God. But this particular majestic God is characterized by *mišpāṭ ûṣĕdāqâ,* the exercise of authority in a way that reflects what is right, not least in light of relationships with the community. Yahweh thus redefines the meaning of holiness.

9

Israel and Judah

Yahweh's first actual words in Isaiah are that expostulation, "Children I reared, brought up, and they—they rebelled against me!" Whereas a domestic animal acknowledges its owner,

> Israel does not acknowledge,
> my people does not pay attention.
> Hey, nation that comes short,
> a people heavy with waywardness,
> Offspring who act badly,
> children who act ruinously!
> They have abandoned Yahweh,
> spurned Israel's Holy One,
> become quite estranged. (Is 1:2-4)

In Isaiah, Israel can thus be identified with Judah, which is a little paradoxical, because in the eighth century "Israel" is the name of Judah's northern neighbor (cf. Is 7:1). The context of Isaiah 17:4-11 indicates that "Jacob" also refers to the northern kingdom in that passage (so also, for instance, Is 9:8 [7]). But Isaiah usually calls the northern kingdom "Ephraim" (e.g., Is 7:2-9, 17; 11:13; 28:1-4) and uses "Israel" more as a theological term than a political one. It denotes "my people" (Is 1:2). For practical purposes, in Isaiah Judah therefore *is* Israel. That establishes Judah's status. It is the embodiment of the people of Yahweh.

That fact could imply that Judah rather than Ephraim is the real Israel. The same question arises in Isaiah 40–55, where addressing "Jacob-Israel" might imply that the addressees (the exiles? the people in Jerusalem? a faithful group within the wider community?) are the real Israel (as the other group is not). But the context points in another direction. Whoever are the addressees, they are people who have a hard time believing that they are Yahweh's people, or believing that this designation means anything any longer. The prophet's point is not "they are not Jacob-Israel; it is you who are" but "you are not nothing; you are Jacob-Israel" or "you can't get away with your waywardness; you are Jacob-Israel." "You as Israel are my servant, as Jacob you are the one I chose, as Abraham's offspring you are my friend" (Is 41:8). So Israel need not share the fear of other peoples as Cyrus advances, even though it feels as feeble as a worm. As Yahweh's servant, Jacob-Israel then has a vocation to fulfill, as the means of Yahweh's governance becoming known to the world (Is 42:1-4). Its very existence is designed to show the world what Yahweh's covenant means, and thus to bring light to nations (Is 42:5-9).

The trouble is, there is no way it can fulfill such a vocation. This servant is deaf and blind (Is 42:18-25). It is itself in prison and it will not see why. That incapacity does not mean Yahweh abandons it. It is, after all, a people for whom Yahweh gave up an interest in Egypt or its acolytes, because it was valuable in Yahweh's eyes, the object of Yahweh's love; and that love still holds (Is 43:3-4). Yahweh intends to bring the Israelites back from the four corners of the world (Is 43:5-7). Yahweh's sacrifice of Egypt for Israel came to its climax at the Reed Sea, and Yahweh intends to do something analogous now, something that makes it simultaneously possible both to remember the past and to forget it because the new event eclipses it for this generation (Is 43:16-21). Yahweh's acts at creation and at the Reed Sea are thus encouragements to believe and hope now (Is 51:9-16). Yahweh is acting now, as then, as Israel's creator and restorer. They are faint (Is 40:29), but Yahweh's servant knows how to aid the faint (Is 50:4). The people longing for Yahweh to act in faithfulness and to deliver them need to look to Abraham and Sarah for evidence that Yahweh can do so, and to see that Yahweh's concern for the nations is part of the significance of their deliverance (Is 51:1-8). Blind and deaf as the Israelites are, Yahweh still intends them to function as witnesses to what

Yahweh has said and done. Indeed, in a sense their incapacity puts them in an even better position so to witness. So their restoration will be a means of nations coming to acknowledge Yahweh (Is 49:7). Jacob-Israel becomes a covenant for people precisely through Yahweh's raising the land by bringing its former inhabitants home (Is 49:8-13). The Israelites are Yahweh's servants. They enjoy the everlasting commitment and covenant promised to David, and corporately they now play David's role (Is 54:17b–55:5). Their going home will be a sign that will stand forever (Is 55:12-13). They will be called "the holy people, the ones restored by Yahweh" (Is 62:11).

Not only so; Yahweh's insistence on staying committed to them is something that will at last turn them from disbelief to trust, from rebellion to acknowledgment, from blindness to sight (Is 43:8-13). Yahweh is committed to turning Jacob, to stopping Israel withdrawing (Is 49:5; contrast Is 6:10), and he still plans that servant Israel should fulfill its calling. Yahweh intends to raise Jacob's clans, to turn Israel's shoots (Is 49:6); "clans" indicates reference to the whole people, and the language suggests a restoration that is both religious and physical. The exiles must leave Babylon and stay clear of anything taboo as they carry Yahweh's vessels (Is 52:11). Their exodus will be one better than the exodus from Egypt; they will not have to hurry, because Yahweh goes before them and protects their rear (Is 52:12).

Isaiah 63:7–64:12 [11] then retells Israel's story. Yahweh made a commitment to this household at the beginning in the conviction that they would be faithful, and so he got involved with them in their troubles and delivered them. "But they—they rebelled and hurt his holy spirit, and he changed into their enemy." So their more recent history has known nothing of the way Yahweh delivered them in Egypt and at the Reed Sea and brought them into the land. Abraham or Israel would hardly recognize them. Yet on the basis of that earlier experience they can call on Yahweh to act this way again, to act as father and restorer. But they know the instinct to rebel, so they also have to ask Yahweh to stop them straying (Is 64:5-7 [4-6] puts even more strongly the conviction that it is Yahweh's action or inaction that makes them sinners).

Israel's waywardness lies in being unwilling to listen to Yahweh's teaching and in telling their prophets that they want to hear delusion, not truth (Is

30:9-11). They want their prophets to get out of the way, which also means getting out of *the* way, Yahweh's way. Their inclination to worship other deities appears in the book's opening chapter and again near its close (Is 1:29; 65:1-12; 66:3-4). They want to hear no more of Israel's Holy One. They call themselves by the name Israel but not in truth or faithfulness (Is 48:1-8). The exiles are tough people who take a huge amount of turning. This toughness was why in the past Yahweh declared intentions before fulfilling them, so that they would not be able to attribute them to their images, and also why Yahweh also says new things in the context of the exile, so that they cannot say Yahweh only spoke in the past (Is 48:1-8).

As well as underscoring its status, designating them "Israel" underscores the seriousness of their waywardness. The bard of Isaiah 5:1-6 addresses the people of "Jerusalem" and "Judah" about the vineyard that will be ravaged for its fruitlessness, but then (turning prophet) goes on,

> Because the household of Israel is the vineyard of Yahweh Armies,
> and the people of Judah are the plant he delighted in.
> He expected the exercise of authority, but there—pouring [of blood],
> faithfulness, but there—crying out. (Is 5:7)

Judah is not any old people living a wayward life. It is *Israel,* "Yahweh's vineyard." The consequences of its failure have already been described. It resembles a man who has been mugged, and yet it refuses to learn its lesson and in fact continues to come back for more (Is 1:5-7). The book also likes to describe Israel-Judah as (the household of) Jacob (e.g., Is 2:5, 6; 44:21, 23; 58:1), which reminds us that Jacob-Israel was an actual person, and there is occasionally a hint that the character of Jacob is reflected in the behavior of his descendants, and of the same being true of Judah's character (e.g., Is 48:1).

Yet Yahweh has a servant who is in a position to intercede with Yahweh on their behalf (Is 53:1-12). Yahweh wipes out their rebellions and declines to think about their failures. But Yahweh does that "for my own sake" (Is 43:25) because of who he is as one who carries people's wrongdoing and because he wants to safeguard his good name. It is on this basis that the prophecy urges people to turn back to Yahweh (Is 44:22).

10

Jerusalem and Zion Critiqued and Threatened

The opening "vision" in Isaiah concerns "Judah and Jerusalem," and the entire book has Jerusalem-Zion as a central focus. While the expression "holy city" does not yet have all the resonances it will later gain, it is significant that the phrase first comes in Isaiah (Is 48:2; 52:1; the other Old Testament occurrences are Neh 11:1, 18 and Dan 9:24). Given that *holy* is a word that denotes Yahweh's supernatural nature, it is may seem surprising to find the word attached to a city or a people. But when Yahweh lays hold on something, it ceases to be so ordinary. Among other implications, you can't mess with it.

In Isaiah 51:16, Zion is uniquely described as "my people." In Isaiah, Jerusalem-Zion (like "servant") is a tensive symbol, capable of having more than one referent. It can denote a location, or a physical city, or the people who live in the city, or the corporate personality of the city (we talk in similar terms of London or New York). It can also refer to that corporate personality as a metaphysical entity that in some sense exists independently of its population, and (in contrast) perhaps to the people of the city who are living elsewhere but who identify with it. But whereas "Jerusalem" can be used as a down-to-earth geographical term, "Zion" is always a more dominantly religious or theological term for the place where Yahweh lives. It is Yahweh's living there that makes it holy.

Isaiah 1 again introduces major aspects of this theme. Once more, it starts as bad news. After the desolating of Judah as a whole by Sennacherib,

"Maiden Zion has survived like a shelter in a vineyard, like a hut in a melon field," almost as devastated as Sodom and Gomorrah (Is 1:8-9). Yet this is nothing compared with the devastation that will come with the city's fall in 587, which is unrecorded in the book but presupposed by Isaiah 40–55 and still a reality in Isaiah 56–66.

The bad news regarding the city's experience has at its background the bad news regarding its life. Its Sodom-like experience matches its Sodom-like life (Is 1:10-23). Jerusalem-Zion is significant because the temple is there, and the people have been faithful in their worship in that temple, bringing offerings, celebrating festivals and praying fervently. Isaiah does not accuse them of offering merely formal worship. They meant every hallelujah and every urgent cry for deliverance; there was no mismatch between their inner feelings and the outward expression of their worship. But there was a mismatch between the fervency of their worship and the life the city lived outside worship. When their hands were raised in fervent praise, what Yahweh saw was the blood on those hands. While few people would be directly guilty of murder, the capital city ran the affairs of Judah in a way that enabled it to live well by skillful manipulation of the systems of taxation, law, migration and landholding. Such policies meant ignoring the rights of orphans and widows and depriving subsistence farmers of their means of livelihood, and abandoning any conviction that Yahweh was involved in political events in their day and any attentiveness to Yahweh's teaching or word (cf. Is 5:8-25). So "truthful town," the place where "faithfulness used to stay," has become immoral in its unfaithfulness to Yahweh, and has turned into a place where murderers live (Is 1:21).

So notwithstanding the fervency of their praise and prayer,

> This people has approached me with its mouth, honored me with its lips,
> but kept its heart far from me.
> Their reverence for me has become
> a learned human command. (Is 29:13)

While their heart in the English sense (their emotions) may have been in their worship, there was a disjunction between their heart in the Old Testament sense (their mind or attitude or will) and God's heart. They were very familiar with the words of the worship material, but that familiarity was as far as their reverence for Yahweh went.

The last part of the book similarly critiques the city's people for having recourse to Yahweh for guidance and blessing, and fasting in this connection, but for accompanying their fasting by exploiting fellow members of their own community, so that Yahweh pays no attention to their worship. Better to share their food (and their homes and clothes) than forgo their food (Is 58:1-7).

So how is Yahweh to handle the sin of Jerusalem? Does Yahweh's commitment to the city mean it can always be sure of pardon? Or does Yahweh's commitment to righteousness mean it is bound to be abandoned and destroyed?

The book's opening chapter suggests an interim answer. The country and the city have experienced terrible devastation, but the city has finally been preserved. Yahweh acts in anger against Jerusalem to exact redress for wrongdoing (Is 1:24), as Yahweh did to Sodom. But notwithstanding its failure to wash the blood off its hands (Is 1:16), some leftovers survive; the parallel with Sodom breaks down. The narrative in Isaiah 36–37 fills out this story, which shows Yahweh fulfilling a promise: "I will protect this city and deliver it for my sake and for the sake of David my servant" (Is 37:35)—not because of what its present occupants deserve. Hezekiah himself fills out the argument that lies behind the basis for that promise (e.g., Is 37:15-20).

The prophecies in Isaiah 29 and Isaiah 31 nuance this understanding. In light of its wrongdoing, Yahweh declares the intention to camp against Jerusalem as David once had (Is 29:1-4), notwithstanding the way it keeps the festivals year by year, or perhaps even because it keeps the festivals year by year (cf. Is 29:13). The city looks doomed to fall to Yahweh as it once fell to David. But then there is a great reversal, and Yahweh "attends" to Jerusalem in a positive way. Suddenly the strangers attacking the city disappear like dust or chaff or like a bad dream (Is 29:5-6). To put it another way, Yahweh will descend on Mount Zion like a lion or vulture pouncing on its prey, but will turn out to shield and rescue it (Is 31:4-5).

The book called Isaiah thus has two pieces of bad news to deliver about Jerusalem-Zion. There is bad news about its life, and bad news about its prospects.

11

Jerusalem and Zion Chastised and Restored

The bad news about Jerusalem-Zion's life means that those deliverances cannot and will not be the end of the story. Jerusalem escaped because of Yahweh's mercy, not because such escape was what it deserved. It paid attention to its defences and it looked to its water supply, "but you did not pay attention to the one who did it, you did not look to the one who shaped it long before." Yahweh had summoned people to mourning (at their losses, at the waywardness that caused these, at the further danger this waywardness put them in), but instead they were rejoicing (at their escape, at Yahweh's deliverance, at Yahweh's presence with them) like people who did not acknowledge that another disaster might be on its way tomorrow (Is 22:8-13). "If this waywardness could be expiated for you before you die . . ." Yahweh continues, with the terrible solemnity of an oath that leaves the consequences unstated. The only thing that could make cleansing and reconciliation impossible is the denial that there is a problem and a consequent refusal to have it dealt with. Therefore they have to turn back to Yahweh (Is 31:6).

Then the people of Jerusalem will not continue to weep, because Yahweh will show great grace at the sound of their crying out (Is 30:19-26; both "weep" and "show grace" are repeated). And whenever they leave the path they will hear a voice behind saying, "This is the way, follow it," and they will abandon their images. The rains will fall, crops grow, cattle flourish, brooks flow, sun and moon shine preternaturally; and all on the day of slaughter when towers fall, the day when Yahweh bandages the people's injuries. The image of new growth already appeared in Isaiah 4:2-6, leading into the further promise that the survivors of Yahweh's devastation will be counted as holy. Yahweh in person will have washed the bloodstains off Jerusalem. The burning the city has gone through will be a refining. And henceforth the city will be protected. It thus transpires that its chastisement is not merely punitive but also restorative (Is 1:21-31). Its silver has turned into slag (Is 1:22), but the turning of Yahweh's hand against it is designed to smelt away this slag. More literally,

> I will restore your authorities as at the first,
> your counselors as at the beginning.
> Afterwards you will be called faithful city,
> truthful town.
> Zion will be redeemed with the exercise of authority,
> those in her who turn with faithfulness. (Is 1:26-27)

The destruction of Jerusalem in 587 is unrecorded but presupposed in the book; it is the more radical answer to the question of whether Yahweh will stay long-tempered forever. But that catastrophe, too, cannot be the end of the story. After fifty years of the city's devastation and the exile of many of its people, Yahweh declares that the time of its chastisement is over; the time for its comfort has come. Yahweh intends to return to the city, taking its exiles back with him. The community is withered like grass by Yahweh's searing wind; but Yahweh's word stands forever. Thus there is good news to be proclaimed to Zion-Jerusalem (Is 40:1-11).

Meanwhile, Zion says to itself, "Yahweh left me; my Lord forgot me" (Is 49:14). While the actual people of Jerusalem (whether in exile or in Judah) can be reckoned to have lamented thus, it is the corporate entity that the prophet imagines lamenting, the entity that exists as a person independently of the people who happen to live there at a particular moment. Yahweh denies the charge of putting Zion out of mind and points to the way its exiles are gathering, like her bridal garments. Instead of being short of inhabitants, she will be overwhelmed by them (Is 49:15-26). If Yahweh had divorced Zion and sold its children into servitude, then they could not complain, because there was good reason (Is 50:1). But Yahweh's continuing interest in Zion's children (which contrasts with their unresponsiveness) suggests that divorce is not the right image for what happened to the relationship. Yahweh is still committed to delivering them and has the power to put down the powers of oppression (Is 50:1-3). The city is in a hopeless situation as a result of being the victim of Yahweh's wrath, but Yahweh is now transferring that wrath to its oppressors. It has to believe it is the case, and act like it (Is 51:17–52:6). Its God has begun to reign and is returning (Is 52:7-10). It can shout for joy because it is about to spread right and left, its fear and shame abolished (Is 54:1-16a). Yahweh admits having abandoned it, but he did so only for a short time; he is now reestablishing it and promises not to abandon it again. Yahweh's commitment and covenant will now stand forever. The situation parallels that after the flood, when Yahweh promised not to flood the earth again. The city will become like a woman bejeweled. Its people will now be Yahweh's disciples and will all enjoy well-being and security.

The picture is gloriously developed in Isaiah 60–62. The world is in darkness, but Yahweh's light has dawned on Zion, so that nations can walk by it. Its children are coming from afar. The wealth of the nations is coming from afar, too, for Zion's sake, to declare Yahweh's praise and bring offerings. The coming of that wealth benefits the city and glorifies Yahweh. These foreigners will build the city's walls, and the city will be splendidly appointed. All nations and kings are to serve it. This is "Zion of the Holy One of Israel." It will know Yahweh as its deliverer and restorer. It will be characterized by well-being and faithfulness rather than violence and ruin. Yahweh will be its light, night and day (Is 60:1-22). At the moment it is characterized by weakness, woundedness, captivity and grief, but foreigners will then look after its people's flocks and crops while its people function as Yahweh's priests and servants; their great shame will be replaced by great wealth, and Yahweh will make a permanent covenant commitment to them (Is 61:1-7). The city will be a beautiful crown in Yahweh's hand, no longer forsaken and desolate but delighted in and espoused by Yahweh (Is 62:3-5). Once again Yahweh commissions the clearing of a way for people to come back and for Yahweh to come as deliverer (Is 62:10-11).

How could the city's future be envisioned in any more glorious terms? By picturing it as the creation of a new heavens and new earth (Is 65:17-25). The context makes clear that the prophet is not referring to a literal new cosmos but to a whole new world for this city. "The sound of weeping and the sound of a cry will not make itself heard there again," in contrast to Isaiah 5:7. People will thus live out their lives instead of having them cut short. They will build houses and live in them, plant vineyards and enjoy their fruit, rather than having them destroyed by enemies. Thus "they will not toil to no purpose, they will not bear children to terror." They will have a relationship of living, instant communication with Yahweh, one in which the new creation vision of Isaiah 11:6-9 will be realized. It will indeed be a whole new world.

Isaiah 12 lays out songs for "the population of Zion" to sing "on that day," the day of Yahweh's restoration. Zion is called to give thanks to Yahweh for its deliverance in such a way that all the nations hear. Isaiah 26:1-6 provides another song to sing about Judah's strong city. In the prophet's vision, the city lacks literal walls, but "deliverance is what he makes walls and rampart": who then needs walls? (cf. Zech 2:5-9 [1-5]). The city does have gates, but they are there in the vision in order to be opened for "the faithful nation, the one that guards truthfulness. [Its] intention held firm, you guard it in peace, in peace because it is trustful in you" (Is 26:3). "Yahweh founded Zion; in it the weak of his people can take refuge" (Is 14:32).

The moon will know shame, the sun will know disgrace,
   when Yahweh Armies has begun to reign
On Mount Zion and in Jerusalem,
   and before his elders will be splendor. (Is 24:21-23)

12

The Remains

Thus a further way in which Yahweh can resolve the tension between the demands of faithfulness and the demands of righteousness is to bring calamity on the people (thereby recognizing the demand of righteousness) but to keep the people in being in a reduced form so that it can blossom again (thereby recognizing the demand of faithfulness). The idea of a remnant emerges from that stratagem.

"The remnant" has become a technical theological term, but the Old Testament expression does not start off as one. In English the remains of something are just the leftovers, which is the connotation of *šĕʾār, yeter* and related words. The image starts from the perspective of the entity as a whole and from how things were before, and it emphasizes the scope of the disaster. All that remains is sad leftovers. The associated terms *śārîd, pālîṭ* and related words indicate that something has "survived" or "escaped" the disaster; they hint that all might not be lost.

After a forest fire its "remains" may be so few that a boy can record them; that fact provides an image for the total destruction of Assyria (Is 10:19). With a little exaggeration, Judah can see its own destruction by Sennacherib as coming not much short of that totality, or of the destruction of Sodom; Yahweh allowed only a few survivors (Is 1:8-9; cf. Is 37:4). Talk in terms of leftovers or remains is thus a way of saying that destruction was more or less complete. The leftovers are merely the evidence that there was once something here. Ephraim will be like an emaciated body, or like a field that has been harvested so that there are only gleanings left, or like an olive tree that has been thoroughly beaten so that only a handful of olives "remain" on out-of-reach branches (Is 17:4-6). In the vision of world devastation, "few people remain" and the city remains only as a ruin; the vision repeats the image of the thoroughly beaten olive tree (Is 24:6, 11-12). All that will be left of the people is something like a flagstaff on a mountaintop or a banner on a hill (Is 30:17). "I remained all alone," says abandoned Zion (Is 49:21).

Yet "more or less" is not total. It is not the same as "nothing will be left over" (Is 39:6). If something escapes, there is the potential for a future. It can at least open up the possibility of restoration and renewed growth. In Judah, if there are people who have escaped, then they can be recipients of majesty and glory; if there are remains, if there are leftovers, they can be called "holy" (Is 4:2-3). Yahweh will continue to be associated with them. Yahweh in person can become for these remains a beautiful crown, a glorious diadem (Is 28:5). The remains, the people who escaped, can again take root downward and can again fruit upward (Is 37:31-32). In the exile, there are only the remains of the household of Israel, but they are the people Yahweh addresses and promises to carry (Is 46:3). If there are remains of Yahweh's people in Assyria, Egypt, Babylonia and across the Mediterranean, then Yahweh can reach out to take hold of them, assemble them, make a way home for them (Is 11:11-16).

Thus the preservation of leftovers is an act of mercy. The remains are not people who deserved to survive, any more than Saul of Tarsus deserved to have the Lord appear to him. They are simply the fortunate beneficiaries of the fact that Yahweh is giving scope for mercy to the people as a whole. It is not that people survive because they turn to Yahweh. Rather they must turn to Yahweh because they have survived. For the sake of the future of the people as a whole, the surviving remnant must become the faithful remnant. They must now lean on Yahweh in truth, instead of stupidly leaning on the superpower, and turn to Yahweh (Is 10:20-21).

The book of Isaiah often makes this point without using "remnant" language. For instance, the exiles in Babylon are people who survived the calamity, and are thus a remnant of whom Isaiah 50:10 asks, "Who among you reveres

Yahweh, listens to his servant's voice? One who has walked in deep darkness and had no brightness must trust in Yahweh's name and lean on his God." The words constitute a challenge to the remnant community to become the faithful remnant. The effect might be to constitute a (faithful) remnant within the remnant. And in Isaiah 65:13-16 this remnant within the remnant becomes "my servants." They are the people who "tremble" at Yahweh's word (Is 66:5).

"The leftovers" or "the remains" is thus a usefully ambiguous expression. The first great ambiguity attaches to Isaiah 6:9-13. Yahweh declares that cities are to lie ruined without inhabitants and houses without anyone in them, so that the land is quite deserted. Translations differ in their understanding of how the passage goes on. The New Revised Standard Version continues the soberness as Yahweh continues, "even if a tenth part remain in it, it will be burned again, like a terebinth or an oak whose stump remains standing when it is felled," then adds as apparently the prophet's own footnote, "The holy seed is its stump." In contrast, NJPS has "but while a tenth part yet remains in it, it shall repent. It shall be ravaged like the terebinth and the oak, of which stumps are left even when they are felled: its stump shall be a holy seed." Is this whole closing verse a continuation of the message about disaster? Or does just the last phrase add a note of hope and promise? Or is the whole closing verse a challenge to "what remains" to respond and become the "faithful remnant"?

Similar questions arise in the account of Isaiah's meeting with Ahaz, which follows. Isaiah takes with him his son "Leftovers-will-return" (Is 7:3). Does this name constitute a promise that only remains of Assyria will return home? Or a warning that only remains of Judah will survive? Or a promise that remains of Judah will survive? Or a challenge that the remains of Judah must turn to Yahweh?

Then, after describing how more or less nothing will "remain" of Assyria, Isaiah declares:

> On that day, the remains of Israel, the people who have escaped of Jacob's household, will not again any more lean on the one that hit it, but will lean on Yahweh, Israel's Holy One, in truth. The remains will turn, the remains of Jacob, to God the warrior. Although your people, Israel, may be like the sand of the sea, remains will turn for it. An end is decreed, overflowing with

> faithfulness. Because a decreed end—the Lord Yahweh Armies is effecting it in the midst of the entire land. (Is 10:20-23)

Such talk here of the remains of Israel carries solemn connotations after the preceding reference to the pathetic remains of Assyria. Isaiah has made it clear often enough that virtually total destruction has come and/or will come on Judah. But that initial impression is then put in question by the declaration that these "remains," which are also "people who have escaped" (the parallel phrase puts it more positively), will now "lean" on Yahweh rather than on Assyria. In the context of Isaiah, hardly anything more impressive could be said, because whom one leans on or relies on or trusts in is a key indicator of who one is and how one relates to God.[1] Thus it indeed indicates that the remains "turn" to Yahweh. The surviving remnant has become the faithful remnant. Yet the next sentence returns to the negative connotations of "remains" and "turn," or at least reintroduces the ambiguity of the expressions (NJPS reads even Is 10:21 negatively, "only a remnant shall return"). On one side the prophecy returns to the earlier talk of devastating destruction. Yet on the other it speaks of this devastation overflowing with *ṣĕdāqâ*. Does that overflowing denote Yahweh's faithfulness to the divine nature in its tough aspect, so that the devastation is overwhelming with "retribution" (NJPS)? Or might *ṣĕdāqâ* keep its more usual positive connotation, so that the overwhelming is accompanied or moderated by *ṣĕdāqâ* (cf. Is 1:27)?

Some of this ambiguity may reflect diachronic, textual or redactional factors. Perhaps it was more obvious at the time what Isaiah's son's name implied. Perhaps Isaiah 6:9-13 has suffered textually. Perhaps this passage and Isaiah 10:20-23 have been through a process of development as time has passed and situations have changed. We will never know the answers to those questions, but such hypotheses themselves presuppose that there are theological issues here. Remnant thinking seeks to handle a theological issue. The ambiguity of the eventual form of the text, like the ambiguity of Isaiah's son's name, places questions before the people. They have to decide how to read the ambiguity and how to respond to it.

---

[1]For this particular verb, cf. Is 30:10; 31:1; 50:10; each time it stands in parallelism with Isaiah's more characteristic *bāṭaḥ*, "trust."

13

The Nations

The principle of a remnant applies also to the nations. Convulsions in the Middle East in Old Testament times can mean there will be virtually nothing left of other peoples, as of Israel (Is 14:22, 30; 15:9; 16:14; 17:3; 21:17). Yet the people among the nations who have "escaped" (escaped Cyrus? escaped Babylon?) are urged to "gather and come, come forward all at once"; they need to let events make them recognize the emptiness of their gods, and they now have opportunity to do so in recognizing Yahweh (Is 45:20-25). And in due course those escapees will themselves go to proclaim Yahweh's honor among the nations (Is 66:19).

Such invitations are set in context by the opening promise expressed in the first message about the nations in Isaiah 2:1-4, which is itself in context also the final promise regarding Jerusalem-Zion in Isaiah 1, reaching far beyond the promises of restoration in Isaiah 1:24-28 but building on them. Metaphorically speaking, the mountain where Yahweh's house stands is to be turned into the highest mountain in the world, and its exaltation will draw all the nations,

> So that he may teach us his ways
>   and we may walk in his paths.
> Because from Zion teaching will issue,
>   Yahweh's word from Jerusalem.
> He will exercise authority between the nations,
>   decide for many peoples.

They will beat their swords into plowshares,
their spears into pruning hooks.
Nation will not raise sword against nation;
they will not train for war any more.

Isaiah 1–12 closes with a linked declaration that the whole world is to know of Yahweh's deeds in restoring Zion (Is 12:3-6). That theme is developed in Isaiah 40–55. Confronted by the arrival of Cyrus, the nations are put into a state of panic (Is 41:1-7). But the object of Yahweh's action is that people in general may see and acknowledge that Yahweh has done it (Is 41:20). They are destined to learn about the way Yahweh exercises authority in the world (Is 42:1-4), to have their eyes opened, their imprisonment ended (Is 42:5-9). They are therefore summoned to give praise to Yahweh (Is 42:10-12).

Nations will bring their wealth to Jerusalem in connection with recognizing that God, the only God, is in the city—the God who is capable of hiding and has been doing so, but who is also capable of turning from hiding to delivering and has now been doing so (Is 45:14-15). The prophet imagines them testifying to the way image-makers are shamed by what has happened, while Israel finds deliverance and will never be shamed, because Yahweh will never let Israel down (Is 45:16-17). It is at this point that Yahweh invites or urges the "survivors of the nations," the people who have escaped Babylon's power and/or Cyrus's campaigns, to come near, and invites or urges earth's extremities to turn to Yahweh and find deliverance. Every knee is to bend to Yahweh, acknowledging that faithfulness and might lie in Yahweh (Is 45:20-25).

This proclamation to the nations brings good news to the exiles. Nations and their kings will bring the exiles home, looking after them like nurses and bowing right down as a sign of the subservience that reverses the way things have been (Is 49:22-23). Their captors will end up losing their lives and thus losing their captives (Is 49:24-26). But the fact that "Yahweh has bared his holy arm in the eyes of the nations" and that "all earth's extremities have seen our God's deliverance" (Is 52:10) is good news for the nations themselves too. They are in darkness, but Yahweh's light has dawned on Zion, so they can walk by that light. They bring their wealth there, to declare Yahweh's praise and bring offerings. These foreigners will build the city's walls and serve the city (Is 60:1-22). Indeed, the survivors of the nations go to declare Yahweh's name among other far-off nations. They will bring the exiles back as an offering to Yahweh, and some of them will be priests (Is 66:18-21). "New moon after new moon, sabbath after sabbath, all flesh will come to bow down before me" (Is 66:23). So this good news relates not merely to people's outward circumstances but to their relationship with Yahweh. The many were appalled at Yahweh's servant, but he will sprinkle them, and at him kings will shut their mouths (Is 52:13-15). "By his acknowledgment my servant shows himself faithful to the many, and he carries their waywardnesses. Therefore I will allocate him many. . . . He was the one who carried the shortcoming of many, makes intercession for the rebels" (Is 53:11-12).

Keeping sabbath now becomes the key marker of keeping the covenant, of attaching oneself and ministering to Yahweh, of loving Yahweh and being Yahweh's servants. It thus qualifies foreigners to bring their offerings and prayers in Yahweh's house; for Yahweh who gathers the dispersed of Israel intends to gather yet more in addition to the people already gathered (Is 56:1-8). Foreigners and exiles have the same status; they are all people whom Yahweh is "gathering." Foreigners need not feel that just because of their ethnicity they are the victims of the separation or distinction (*hibdîl*) that Yahweh expects of the holy over against the ordinary or the clean over against the taboo. The fact that eunuchs cannot contribute to Israel's future growth as a people does not disbar them; for foreigners, the prophet declares, Yahweh's house is called a prayer house for all peoples. Any group that wishes to commit itself in covenant to Yahweh can come there.

The poems about particular nations (Isaiah 13–23) approach their destiny from a different angle. These individual nations are ones that in different ways affect Judah. The nations are peoples by whom Judah might be impressed, powers that seemed unassailable but are not, peoples who share Judah's subordination to Assyria or with whom Judah might ally against Assyria. The prophecies thus warn Judah, "Don't even think about it," and for the most part warn Judah of the fate that hangs over these peoples; there is nothing to trust there. Yet the chapters include notes of hope for them. Perhaps even Philistia can prove that the weak find refuge in Zion (Is 14:26-32). The point is more explicit regarding Moab (Is 16:1-5). It is most spectacular regarding Egypt (Egypt, of all people!) (Is 19:16-25), where there will be cities swearing allegiance to Yahweh, an altar to Yahweh in the land, Yahweh answering people's prayers and healing people, a highway to Assyria enabling both peoples to serve Yahweh as "my people" and "my handiwork" alongside Israel as "my possession." Even that old whore Tyre after being put in her place will be able to resume her trade and devote her profits to Yahweh (Is 23:17-18).

After Isaiah 13–23 with its focus on individual nations, Isaiah 24–27 almost entirely lacks such concrete references. In the prophet's vision, "Yahweh is wasting the earth, devastating it" (Is 24:1). In another context *hā'āreṣ* could denote "the land" of Canaan, and "the city" (Is 24:12) could be Jerusalem, but here these have become figures for every land and any city. "The earth" stands in parallelism with "the world" (*tēbēl;* Is 24:4) and "the city" indicates how things will be "in the midst of the peoples" (Is 24:13). Yahweh is angry at all the nations and has given them over to slaughter; at the same time the heavenly army will wither and rot (Is 34:1-4). People who know God is coming to bring redress to their enemies, and thus deliver them, can abandon their fear and start standing tall again (Is 35:3-4).

The earth's devastation has come because it "has become profaned under its inhabitants, because they have transgressed teachings, overstepped laws, broken the ancient covenant" (Is 24:5). Such language applies easily to Israel, but it has been extended to the world as a whole, which is assumed to be the recipient of Yahweh's covenant, to know what Yahweh expects of it, and thus to be guilty for ignoring it (cf. Amos 1:3–2:3; also Gen 9:1-17). The parallel with Israel extends to the notion that such action turns the earth from something that was holy to something that is defiled. The argument is summarized later: "The earth has broken, broken up, the earth has split, split apart, the earth has slipped, slipped down, the earth staggers, staggers about like a drunk, sways like a shelter. Its rebellion will be heavy upon it; it will fall and not rise again" (Is 24:19-20).

In response to the vision in Isaiah 24:1-13, or to its implementation, "those people raise their voice, they resound at Yahweh's majesty, they have cried out from the west" (Is 24:14). Perhaps it is the wayward themselves acknowledging the rightness of Yahweh's intention or Yahweh's action. Devastating the city means Yahweh has proved to be a refuge to the poor and needy in their distress when terrifying foreigners overwhelmed them, and that these strong and terrifying nations must honor Yahweh rather than insisting on their independence (Is 25:1-5).

There is a double contrast between that "city" and "this mountain" (Is 25:6-10a). "This mountain" may be Mount Zion, mentioned not long ago (Is 24:23; cf. Is 2:2-5; 4:2-5; 27:13), though the portrait of what will happen here may better fit the mountain land of Canaan (Is 11:9; 57:13; 65:25). On this mountain Yahweh Armies will arrange the ultimate festival banquet, "for all peoples." On this mountain Yahweh will bring death to an end, for "all peoples . . . all nations," and thus wipe the tears from "all faces"; there will be no more war, no more death, no more mourning. And "from over all the earth" Yahweh will take away the disgrace that Israel has earned for itself through the humiliation Yahweh put it through as a consequence of its waywardness. Whether the mountain is Canaan in general or Zion in particular, Yahweh does not abandon the particularity that characterizes the Scriptures as a whole. Yahweh's plan was to reach the world by relating to Israel in particular; Israel's resistance to Yahweh brought it chastisement and shame, but it is still through Israel that Yahweh fulfils that purpose. Israel has been the very embodiment of "the poor and needy" (Is 25:4), but its shame has been removed as the strong and terrifying nations have been put down, so that it is no longer a weak, pathetic, humiliated little people but the host of this great festival. Moab provides a concrete (and vivid) illustration of Yahweh's devastating the fortified city: in the prophet's vision, "he has humbled its majesty," and "the high fortification of its walls he has laid low and humbled, brought them to the ground, right to the dirt" (Is 25:11-12). Thus Judah will have a song to sing about Jerusalem, whose deliverance and peace issue from and contrast with the laying low and humbling of the lofty town, which the weak and powerless can therefore trample (Is 26:1-6).

Is all this destruction necessary? "As your decisions come about for the earth, the inhabitants of the world learn faithfulness. If grace is shown to the faithless person, he does not learn faithfulness; in the land of uprightness they do wickedness, and do not revere the majesty of Yahweh" (Is 26:9-10). They cannot see Yahweh's hand lifted up and taking action in passion for Israel and consuming Yahweh's enemies. Perhaps they will not look, or perhaps it is not lifted up. Either way they need to see it in order to be put to shame (Is 26:11).

What Yahweh has done previously provides a basis for the conviction that this reversal will come about, and for a plea to establish well-being for Israel (Is 26:12-15). Israel has been subject to masters other than Yahweh, but Yahweh dealt with them and they are now dead and gone, while Yahweh increased Israel and gained honor in the process. Yet the present still contrasts with that past, and Israel needs Yahweh to treat it in a different way from the dead-and-gone ghosts of the nations that will never come to life or get up. "May *your* dead come to life" and "get up"; indeed, the prophet urges them to wake up and resound as Yahweh makes life-giving dew fall on the land of the ghosts (Is 26:19).

The destiny of the nations in relation to Yahweh is thus not so different from Israel's destiny. Like Israel, they are expected to live in light of their knowledge of God's expectations of them in their attitude to God and to one another. Like Israel, they are liable to God's "attending" to them because of the shortcomings in their attitudes. Like Israel, they are liable to be cut down so that little of them remains. Like Israel, it is then open to these remains to turn to Yahweh, and ultimately the nations are indeed destined to turn to the God who lives on Zion and to find their mutual relationships healed there.

14

The Empires and Their Kings

The first three great Middle Eastern empires, Assyria, Babylon and Medo-Persia, have a prominent place in Isaiah. In addition, when Isaiah talks simply about "the nations" this can be a reference to the empire of the day. Thus Yahweh summons "the nations" to chastise Israel (Is 5:26), referring to Assyria; the following cola refer to "them" as "it." "All the nations" are warring on Zion (Is 29:7-8). Yahweh acts against "the nations," which means Assyria is shattered (Is 30:28, 31; the details in verse 28 are unclear). When Yahweh plans to break Assyria, this involves an arm being poised "over all the nations" (Is 14:26). Yahweh similarly sets up a signal for "the nations" to bring Israelite exiles home (Is 11:12; cf. Is 49:22). Threatening Babylon, there can be heard "the uproar of kingdoms, nations assembling" (Is 13:4). From this use of "the nations" to refer to the empire, we might infer such a reference in other passages where there is no direct indication in the context. After the destruction of the great foreign city, "a strong people will honor you, a town of oppressive nations will revere you" (Is 25:3). "The nations count like a drop from a pan. . . . All the nations are as nothing over against him; they count as naught, emptiness to him" (Is 40:15). "All the nations must gather at once, peoples must assemble. Who among them could announce this?" (Is 43:9). Yahweh took Cyrus's hand "to put down nations before him and strip the loins of kings" (Is 45:1). People among the nations who have "escaped" are urged to come and recognize Yahweh (Is 45:20-25). If Yahweh were to tear apart the sky and come down, "nations will tremble at your presence" (Is 64:2 [1]).

Explicitly, Yahweh is involved in the expansionism that turns Assyria into a great empire, drafting its army to fulfill its own instincts in a way that works with Yahweh's intention to devastate Judah (Is 5:26-30). Of course Assyria does not know it acts as Yahweh's agent. It is involved in its expansionism for its own reasons. So "when the Lord has brought to an end all his work against Mount Zion and Jerusalem, 'I will attend to the vast fruit of the king of Assyria's thinking and to the exalted glory of his eyes'" (Is 10:12). Translations commonly refer to pride, but as usual this slants and/or narrows down Isaiah's words in a vague, moralistic direction. Yahweh's point is that the king had had vast ambitions, had achieved them and had thus gained unparalleled respect and esteem in his world and also in his own assessment. He was indeed proud of what he had achieved by his power and insight, moving peoples' borders, plundering their treasuries and exiling their populations (and he had grounds for his pride), but he had thus come to see himself as more important than the one whose unwitting agent he was. It is for this reason that Yahweh will put him in his place (Is 10:13-19; cf. Is 10:24-27, 33-34; 14:24-27; 30:29-33; 31:8-9). He did not see his achievement in the context of Yahweh's purpose but only as his own achievement, scoffing at the idea that Yahweh could deliver Jerusalem (Is 36:18-20) in a way that amounted to ridicule (*ḥārap;* Is 37:4, 10, 17) as he stirred himself up against Yahweh (*rāgaz* hitpael; Is 37:22-29).

The center of the poems about the nations (Is 17:12-14) applies to "many peoples, that roar like the seas' roaring," language applied to Assyria in Isaiah 8:7. Yahweh shouts them down, and they flee. In evening they inspired terror; by morning they have gone, just like Assyria in Isaiah 36:1–37:37. Assyria becomes a figure for any such threat (Babylon, Persia, Greece, Rome, Turkey, Britain, the USA, etc.).

It will be through Babylon that Yahweh brings about Assyria's final downfall and also Judah's fall. But then Yahweh will attend to Babylon (Is 13:1). In this connection Yahweh speaks of having summoned warriors from kingdoms and nations to destroy the whole earth for its waywardness in an event that will bring darkness over the whole earth, putting down the humanly impressive. He calls them "sanctified" warriors, because he is calling and dedicating them to their task (even though they don't know that they are thus serving him). By means of them, he says, "I will put an end to the majesty of the aggressive and the majestic position of the oppressors" and decimate the world's peoples (Is 13:2-16). There is no reference to a specific empire; it is the context that indicates that Babylon's downfall will be a concretion of this event. Thus the relationship between historical and ultimate is the converse of the one in Isaiah 17:12-14. There the particular gives a way of thinking about the ultimate; here the movement is the reverse. It is against the background of the generic declaration that Isaiah 13:17-22 speaks more concretely about the Medes as the people who will shatter Babylon in its splendor and majesty and turn it into something resembling Sodom and Gomorrah. In this context, there is a particular reason for doing so:

> Because Yahweh will have compassion on Jacob
> and again choose Israel and settle them on their soil.
> Strangers will join them,
> attach themselves to Jacob's household.
> Peoples will take them
> and bring them to their place.
> The household of Israel will possess them on Yahweh's soil
> as servants and handmaids.
> They will become captors of their captors
> and will rule over their oppressors. (Is 14:1-2)

The destiny of empires relates in negative and in positive ways to Yahweh's involvement with Israel.

When Yahweh gives them relief from the pain and turmoil of their oppression under Babylon, they will be in a position to declaim a poem over its king. One expects such a funeral address to take the form of a eulogy, but this one takes the form of mockery, directed at a king who is still very much alive at the moment (Is 14:4-11). It rejoices in the fact that Yahweh has broken the club or staff (the words used of Assyria in Is 10:5) that struck peoples. They thus now cheer in relief; down in Sheol other dead kings prepare to greet this new arrival who will join them in their fall from majesty to insignificance. A parallel dyslogy then compares the Babylonian king to Venus, the morning star, that rises as if seeking to ascend to glory each morning but then disappears when outshone by the sun as it rises. In place of the splendor of a world emperor, the king will have an ignominious death without proper burial and thus without a proper resting place (Is 14:12-21).

The fate of the king is mirrored in the fate of the city itself (Is 14:22-23). Babylon falls like a woman falling from her position of authority in the household. It had shown no compassion and it had assumed that it would always be in its position of power, thinking it had all the information resources it needed to cope with any threats or crises, but it turns out to be wrong (Is 47:1-15).

So one empire gives way to another, and one great king gives way to another. Cyrus no more acknowledges Yahweh than Sennacherib or Nebuchadnezzar had done, yet this neglect no more stops Yahweh giving him victories than was the case with Assyrian and Babylonian kings. Indeed, this action is designed (among other things) to lead to such acknowledgment by Cyrus and by the world from east to west (Is 45:3-6).

15

Divine Sovereignty and Human Responsibility

The account of Yahweh's relationship with Assyria presupposes an approach to the interweaving of divine sovereignty and human responsibility. Yahweh summons the Assyrian army (Is 5:26). The club or staff it wields is the means of Yahweh's anger finding expression (Is 10:4). Yet Assyria is subject to critique for its action, because it is not committed merely to being Yahweh's means of acting against godless Ephraim; it aims to devastate a whole series of nations (Is 10:7-8). It treats Jerusalem and Samaria as just two more nations like these others, their worship of Yahweh just like the worship of other Middle Eastern cities (Is 10:9-11). It rejoices in the impressiveness and splendor of its achievements, in its power and proficiency, as if it were more than a tool in the hand of a craftworker (Is 10:12-15). Therefore it will have to be put down the same way as Ephraim and Judah (Is 10:16-19). While the empire is a means of Yahweh's acting, it is responsible to act in a moral way, to recognize the specialness of Yahweh, and not to become too impressed with itself.

Divine sovereignty and human responsibility interweave in different ways in the relationship between Yahweh and Judah, where there is direct communication between the two parties. Yet Isaiah supports warnings to Judah with strong expressions such as "because Yahweh's mouth has spoken," a way of saying "so what I just said really will happen." There is no (longer) a place for human responsibility here. "The Lord sent a word on

Jacob, it fell on Israel" (Is 9:8 [7]), and it meant devastation. Yahweh's word is performative and not merely informative. The same point is made by the past-tense verbs that Isaiah often uses to describe events that have not yet happened (e.g., Is 2:9; 3:1; 5:13-16; 9:2-7 [1-6]). Yahweh's sovereignty is underscored in another way by the commission to Isaiah and by Isaiah's analysis of the people's position:

Go and say to this people,
"Keep listening, but do not pay attention,
keep looking, but do not acknowledge."
Stiffen the people's attitude,
block its ears, seal its eyes,
Lest it look with its eyes and listen with its ears
and its mind pays attention and it turns and finds healing for itself.
(Is 6:9-10)

Yahweh has poured over you
the spirit of a coma.
He has shut your eyes, prophets,
covered your heads, seers.
The vision of everything has become to you
like the words of a sealed book. (Is 29:10-11)

It is quite understandable that Yahweh should act thus as part of punishing Israel for its intransigence; Jesus' application of Isaiah 6:9-10 (Mk 4:10-12) fits this understanding. Yet taking such words literally introduces an air of unreality into the prophet's ministry. Sharing such words with the people is part of an attempt to gain a response rather than an explanation of why they do not respond, though for readers of the book it provides a framework for reflecting on the failure of the prophet's ministry. The words constitute one further attempt to shake people to their senses. Similar implications underlie that frightening declaration in Isaiah 22:14, "If this waywardness could be expiated for you before you die . . ." Perhaps such a horrific warning can shake people out of their stupor. Again, the prophet subsequently declares, "I have heard annihilation decreed from the Lord Yahweh Armies upon the whole land" (Is 28:22). Yet the context urges people not to scoff at the warning, which suggests that this decree is not final. While Yahweh's speech is thus not only informative but performative, it is capable of being performative in more than one way. It has the intention and may have the effect of making people turn to Yahweh, in which case it has done its work and does not need to be implemented in its direct sense.

Divine sovereignty is thus a subtler affair than it at first seems. A dialectical relationship obtains between divine decision making and human decision making. While nothing happens outside Yahweh's control or outside parameters Yahweh lays down, and some things happen because Yahweh makes explicit decisions, many things happen in part because human beings respond to Yahweh in the way that they do. Jerusalem has to wash the blood from its hands in the sense that it has to change its way of life so that its hands do not become covered in blood (Is 1:15-20), even though Yahweh also promises to wash the stains from Jerusalem (Is 4:4).

Yahweh's promises of restoration from exile also put the emphasis on divine sovereignty. It is simply Yahweh's will to bring it about; it bears no relationship to what the people deserve. Yet it presupposes that people will respond to Yahweh's word and/or to Yahweh's action; there is, after all, "no well-being for the faithless" (Is 48:22). This fact is underscored in Isaiah 56–66, where that warning recurs (Is 57:21). Implicitly, this principle provides some explanation of why the restoration has fallen short of its promises. When people share their food, their homes and their clothes, and keep the sabbath, that is when they will find light and healing, the manifestation of Yahweh's faithfulness and splendor, Yahweh's response to their call and Yahweh's guiding, the rebuilding of the city and the full possession of the land (Is 58:6-14). The fact that Yahweh's arm is not raised in action to deliver does not mean it is incapable of doing so or that Yahweh's ears are deaf, or it means only that those ears are deliberately deaf. Whereas nothing separates foreigners from Yahweh, the people's own waywardness, deception and bloodshed does so for them, making Yahweh's face turn away. And that is why Yahweh's *mišpāṭ* and *ṣĕdāqâ* are far away from them (Is 59:1-15a). Yahweh is displeased that no one is acting to deliver the people (like Cyrus in an earlier context?), and so determines to act in person, as had happened at the Reed Sea. He will impose requital on far-off lands; thus he "will come to Zion as restorer, to people who turn from rebellion in Jacob" (Is 59:16b-20; cf. Is 63:1-6). That last colon gives a new twist to the entire promise. Yahweh is committed to *mišpāṭ ûṣĕdāqâ;* they have to be so committed, too, if they are to be the beneficiaries of such action.

It would be a mistake to make Yahweh's act of restoration conditional on people's turning to Yahweh. But it does require such turning as a response, otherwise the whole project fails. Yahweh's sovereignty is the ultimate factor in events; Yahweh's patience, persistence, resourcefulness and readiness for self-sacrifice mean it will eventually win out. But people have to do their turning, now or in response to Yahweh's act, and that turning makes a difference to the way Yahweh's intention finds its fulfillment.

16

Divine Planning and Human Planning

Talk in terms of divine and human planning constitutes another way of discussing the divine and human role in history. Isaiah does not speak of Yahweh having a plan for the whole of world history, for the whole of Israel's story or for the lives of individuals, but it does speak of Yahweh having plans about what to do at particular moments or in particular connections, and of an overall intent that goes back centuries. Yahweh's plans serve a purpose that goes back to Abraham. While Abraham is explicitly mentioned only four times in Isaiah (Is 29:22; 41:8; 51:2; 63:16), and implicitly referred to twice more (Is 41:2-3, 25), these mentions are more than the rest of the Prophets put together. Yahweh's acts of restoration issue from that purpose. Yahweh who is with the last was also the first.

And in particular and changing contexts, Yahweh plans as a farmer does. There is a time for plowing and a time for sowing, and there are different tools for different tasks. The farmer knows this fact, and his insight comes from Yahweh. It follows that Yahweh operates with the same insight, sometimes plowing, sometimes sowing. "He has made his planning wonderful, made his insight great" (Is 28:23-29).

For instance,

> Yahweh Armies has sworn, saying:
> if it has not happened as I designed . . .

As I have planned, that will take place:
breaking Assyria in my land, trampling on him on my mountains. . . .
This is the plan that is planned for all the earth. . . .
because Yahweh Armies has planned; who could frustrate? (Is 14:24-27)

Isaiah speaks of a royal prince carrying a name that declares, "An-extraordinary-planner-is-the-warrior-God" (Is 9:6 [5]). Like "Yahweh-is-deliverance" or "Remains-will-turn" or "God-is-with-us," this name makes the political affirmation Isaiah presses on the rulers of his day. Yahweh is the one who makes plans and implements them; the politicians need to take account of that fact. Yahweh's devastating "the city" is an instance. The prophet responds to the vision of this event, reflecting that name from Isaiah 9:6 [5], "you have done a wonder, plans from long before, truth, truthfulness" (Is 25:1-2).

Isaiah does recognize that it is the responsibility of politicians to make plans. Yahweh's threat to take away planners along with prophets, elders and other leaders (Is 3:3) presupposes that they are in principle legitimate means whereby the community is directed. The same assumption is implied in the promise that Yahweh will in due course restore good planners to Jerusalem (Is 1:26) and that the shoot from Jesse's stump will have a spirit of planning (Is 11:2).

The trouble is that human planning usually proceeds on the basis of what can be humanly discerned and managed. Syria and Ephraim make such a plan to lean on Judah to join them in rebelling against Assyria (Is 7:5). When we bring God into the picture, plans like those of Syria and Ephraim can be scorned (Is 8:10). All Babylon's planning may get it nowhere (Is 47:13).

The story of Sennacherib's invasion (Is 36:1–37:38) discusses these issues with some irony. Sennacherib asks about the basis for the Judahites' trust that they will be able to resist the Assyrians by means of their planning. Are they trusting in Egypt, or in Yahweh? Egypt will let them down, and Yahweh is the one who has sent Sennacherib and will not save them—indeed, he implies, cannot. But with that slur, Sennacherib digs his grave.

In the context of Sennacherib's invasion, Isaiah urges the nation to take it easy and relax, but this simple advice seems ridiculous (Is 28:11-13). They are convinced that they have to take responsibility for the city's safety, but their action is calculated to have the opposite effect. They have made an alliance with neighbors such as Egypt against Assyria, and they think they have thereby come to an arrangement with the forces of death. Making Egypt their refuge and shelter is an act of blasphemy. Yahweh is supposed to be their refuge, their shelter. There is a place of security in Zion, but it does not lie in bulwarks of stone that the defenders erect. The key to their destiny lies in trusting Yahweh, not in physical defenses. They will find that their alternative refuge or shelter is totally deceptive. The forces of death are actually going to overwhelm them. A few horses and chariots to ride into battle may look a safer bet than trusting Yahweh, but this more plausible policy will not work (Is 28:14-20; 30:15-17). "He too is insightful, but he has brought disaster, and not revoked his word," and "the Egyptians are human beings, not God; their horses are flesh, not spirit. When Yahweh stretches out his arm, the helper will stumble and the one helped will fall; all of them will come to an end together" (Is 31:2-3).

But the natural temptation of politicians is to scorn alternative plans such as ones that involve God (Is 5:19). Judah's rebellion lies in making plans that do not come from Yahweh, and thus piling wrong on wrong (Is 30:1-7). Specifically, it sends envoys to Egypt without asking Yahweh's opinion. That omission is sensible in its way, because Yahweh would say no, on the grounds that they are seeking protection, shelter, refuge, help in Egypt; again, these are words that properly apply solely to Yahweh. Their mission will issue only in shame and disgrace.

After the exile, trust and submission to Yahweh's planning remain a key consideration, though Isaiah 40:27-31 now makes Yahweh's being the creator the key to trust and to finding new strength. When they are told that Yahweh intends to use Cyrus as the means of restoring Jerusalem, the prophet imagines people responding, "You can't do that!" and retorts by asking them to reconsider who is the potter and who is the clay (Is 45:9-13). They have to give up looking at things their own way. "Your plans are not my plans and my ways are not your ways," Yahweh reminds them (the common translation "thoughts" for *maḥăšābôt* is too imprecise); indeed there is as great a gap between their ways and plans and Yahweh's as there is between the sky and the earth (Is 55:8-11).

Two planners and two sets of plans thus keep confronting each other in this book. Yahweh is doing wonders for Judah, but in the short term they are unpleasant wonders through which "the insight of the insightful will perish, the discernment of the discerning will hide" (Is 29:14). These planners are people "who go deeper than Yahweh to hide their plan, and whose deed happens in the dark, and who say 'Who sees us? Who recognizes us?'" as if they were clay that could operate independently of its potter (Is 29:15-16). But the day will come when people will treat the Holy One as holy and be in awe of Israel's God, with a reverence that will go along with or issue from a recognition of true discernment by people who currently err in spirit (Is 29:22-24).

17

David

S*o Isaiah assumes that Judah needs leadership.* Therefore a horrific aspect of its ruining is Yahweh's removing its leadership and replacing it with people who are incompetent in the sense that they cannot safeguard moral and social order (Is 3:1-12). Yet the reason for this action is that the leadership is itself oppressive (Is 3:13-15; cf. Is 9:14-17 [13-16]). A city needs lookouts to guard it and a flock needs shepherds, but this people's lookouts/shepherds are too drunk to see anything (Is 56:9-12).

The prophecy about Shebna and Eliakim, Hezekiah's most senior ministers (Is 22:15-25; cf. Is 36:3), is particularly far reaching. It censures Shebna for commissioning an impressive memorial, in which actually he will never be buried, and it declares that Eliakim will replace him in his position. But he will give way, too, along with the political affairs that depend on him. Whenever a leader is replaced, huge hopes are pinned on his successor, and regularly they are disappointed. Every British and US election illustrates the point.

"Listen, household of David," Isaiah says to Ahaz when the king resists the prophet's attempt to manipulate him into policies that will presuppose trust in Yahweh (Is 7:13; cf. Is 7:2). There are promises attaching to David's household that its present representative is supposed to live by. But Ahaz does not want to be driven into taking that risk. Hezekiah models a different stance in the stories about him. By implication he does so in the reforms the Rabshakeh refers to (Is 36:7), he does so in his attitude to Isaiah (Is 37:2-4), he does so in his recourse to Yahweh for the nation (Is 37:1,

14-20). In a way, he does so for himself, in refusing to accept Yahweh's word as final (Is 38:1-22), though we have noted that these stories about God's involvement in Hezekiah's life are more equivocal.

To judge from Isaiah 32:1-8, there is another problem about the people's leadership. Yahweh there promises a day when a king will reign and leaders will lead in a way that involves the faithful exercise of authority. They will be protectors for people who need protection, they will be people with insight and a capacity to listen (to God, to the cry of the needy?), they will be thoughtful and articulate in the way they speak (of God?), they will be people who live by principle. The implication is that not much of that description is true of Judah's leadership at the time this promise was given.

This promise is not associated with Yahweh's commitment to David. Neither is there any indication that the baby referred to in Isaiah 7:14 is to be born to the royal family, or if it is, that it is a child who will eventually sit on the throne. The emphasis of the passage lies elsewhere, on the child's significance as a sign that Yahweh can be trusted. In contrast, the vision in Isaiah 9:2-7 [1-6] is associated with David. It speaks in the past tense as if the birth of a child to reign on David's throne has already happened, and one might associate it with the birth of Hezekiah. But the passage as a whole cannot be read as referring to events that have already happened, and we have noted that sometimes prophets use the past tense as a sign that something that is chronologically still future is real, because God has determined it. Whoever the child is, his birth promises that the darkness of defeat and destruction that has afflicted the land will come to an end, and that permanent peace and the faithful exercise of authority in the land will become realities. The child's name is "An-extraordinary-planner-is-the-warrior-God; the-everlasting-Father-is-an-officer-for-well-being." This is not a description of the child himself, any more than is the case with other names such as "Yahweh-is-deliverance" or "Remains-will-turn" or "God-is-with-us." It is a statement of what his reign will prove about Yahweh, as Yahweh delivers and blesses the people.

The further David passage in Isaiah 11:1-10 explicitly relates to a future figure and is thus the nearest thing to a messianic prophecy in Isaiah. It presupposes that the Davidic tree has been felled. Yet a felled tree can sometimes produce new shoots and grow again, and Isaiah promises that this will happen to the Davidic tree. And this David will manifest the best qualities of a king such as Hezekiah and of the kingly ideal expressed in Psalm 72, ruling with wisdom, reverence for Yahweh and a decisiveness that protects the weak and poor and sees that the faithless get put down. In the context, the subsequent picture of harmony in the animal world is another promise of the way people who are by nature inclined to feed off others live in harmony with them. Further, "on that day Jesse's root that is standing as a standard to peoples—nations will have recourse to him, and his abode will be glorious" (Is 11:10).

The Davidic idea appears in a quite a different form in Isaiah 44:24–45:7. It portrays Yahweh working through Persia in the way he had worked through Assyria, but it makes the point in more scandalous terms. Cyrus is "my shepherd" and "my anointed." It had indeed been David whom Yahweh anointed to shepherd Israel (e.g., 1 Sam 16; 2 Sam 5:2; 7:7), and when there are no Davidic kings on Israel's throne, Isaiah 11:1-10 encourages Israel to look forward to a day when they would shepherd Israel again. Here Yahweh declares that the pagan king is the one anointed to do this shepherding. David had commissioned the building of Jerusalem and of the temple; now Cyrus will do so. Yahweh had led David to great victories over foreign nations; now Yahweh will so lead Cyrus. Even more scandalously, Cyrus is the one Yahweh loves or espouses and has summoned (Is 48:14-15); the Scriptures do not speak of Yahweh loving David.[1]

Further passages also deconstruct the Davidic idea. The picture of the servant in Isaiah 52:13–53:12 has Davidic resonances, including exalted majesty and a spectacular anointing, though in general the picture contrasts with the kingly ideal of someone handsome like David, for whom all the girls would fall (1 Sam 16:12; 18:6). No one falls for this servant. Here Yahweh's purpose is achieved through someone who is nothing like David.

[1]David was, of course, a man "after God's heart" (1 Sam 13:14), but that expression is not a way of talking about love in Scripture. It means he was someone whom God formulated the intention to choose in order to use in his service. Second Samuel 12:24 does explicitly say that God loved Solomon.

Then Yahweh promises that Israel as a whole is to have a David-like role in the world (Is 54:17b–55:5). Whereas David had been the means of manifesting Yahweh's power in the world, now Israel will be the means of drawing the world to acknowledge Yahweh, in accordance with the promise to Abraham. In keeping with this reformulation, Isaiah 56–66 develops the emphasis on the way Israel will draw people to itself, to Jerusalem and to Yahweh, and ignores David; the point is underscored by the prophet's testimony to anointing (Is 61:1).

Isaiah thus constitutes a microcosm of the complex scriptural attitude to monarchy and to messianism. The Old Testament both accepts and rejects the notion of kingship. It both works with and sidesteps the notion of a Messiah. And Jesus both accepts the idea that he is the Messiah and warns that it is misleading.

18

Yahweh's Day

In Isaiah, as in the Old Testament in general, the broader notion of the End or of Yahweh's day is much more prominent than the gift of a new David.

The word *eschatological* has been applied to some of the book's prophecies, though it is a tricky word.[1]

1. Eschatology can refer to the destiny of the individual, the people of God, the world as a whole and the cosmos. Isaiah has nothing to say about what happens to individuals after they die, beyond its references to death and Sheol, and little to say about any transformation of the cosmos. It focuses on God's ultimate purpose for the world and for Israel.
2. Eschatology may think in terms of an end after which there will be nothing, or in terms of historical experience giving way to an era of timeless blessing, or in terms of our era of flawed history and experience giving way to a new, wholesome era of history and experience. The book called Isaiah promises that Yahweh's act of judgment will lead into Yahweh reigning on Mount Zion and in Jerusalem and into people's enjoyment of human life in fullness.
3. Eschatology can involve the belief that God is putting his ultimate purpose into effect now, through events that can be seen in the world, so that it is already being actualized or realized, or the belief that God

[1] I adapt the paragraphs that follow from my commentary on Isaiah 56–66 mentioned in the acknowledgments.

will do so at some time in the future by means that we cannot at the moment see. Both perspectives appear in Isaiah.

4. While eschatology implies a radical distinction between this age and a coming age, it can see the coming of this new age as gradual, or as involving a dramatic transformation, reversal or discontinuity. The book called Isaiah thinks in terms of dramatic transformation.

5. Eschatology can imply a future that is imminent or one that is far away. Both perspectives appear in Isaiah.

The word *apocalyptic* is another tricky word. Applied to parts of Isaiah, it denotes the forms of eschatology that stress the radical difference between this age and the coming age, the radical nature of the action of God that will bring in the new age, and an associated emphasis on disaster rather than any renewal aspect to what God will do. But apocalyptic can also imply the use of vivid imagery and symbolism, particularly to communicate the nature of this coming calamity.

Much of Isaiah focuses on extraordinary things Yahweh is planning to do in the lives of the prophecies' hearers, and it can speak of these events as the coming of Yahweh's day. "Yahweh Armies has a day against everything majestic and lofty," trees and mountains, towers and walls and ships. "Human majesty will bow, mortal loftiness fall down, and Yahweh alone will stand high, on that day" (Is 2:12-17). The prophet thus threatens the Judah of his time with great calamity. "On that day" Yahweh will whistle for troublemakers from Egypt and Assyria and the land will be devastated (Is 7:18-25).

In keeping with such warnings, other prophecies declare that "in a little while" Yahweh's wrath will have exhausted itself and will be turned on Assyria (Is 10:24-26) and "in a little while" renewal will come for Judah (Is 29:17). "On that day" nature will be transformed, the deaf will hear, the blind will see, and the weak and needy will increase their joy in Yahweh, because the people who terrify them, scoff at them and manipulate the legal system against them will be gone (Is 29:18-21). When Yahweh delivers Jerusalem, "on that day" people will reject the images they have made (Is 31:7). "On that day the leftovers of Israel, the people who escaped in the household of Jacob, will not again lean on the one who struck them, but will truly lean on Yahweh, Israel's Holy One" (Is 10:20). In some of these passages, "on that day" functions chiefly to make a link with what precedes; the time it denotes is thus implicitly rather than explicitly imminent. Further, such passages are often reckoned to come from a later time than other prophecies in their context, though this possibility makes little difference to the theological issue they raise, as they are still promising that such events will take place "soon."

Other victims of Yahweh's army than Israel are similarly bidden to "howl, because Yahweh's day is near; it will come like destruction from the Destroyer" (Is 13:6).

> There: Yahweh's day has come/is coming,
> fierce, with wrath and angry burning,
> To turn the earth into a desolation
> and destroy its sinners from it.
> Because the stars in the heavens and their constellations
> will not shine their light.
> The sun will be dark at its rising,
> the moon will not diffuse its light.
> I shall attend upon the world its evil,
> and upon rebels their waywardness.
> I shall bring to an end the majesty of the arrogant,
> the majesticness of the terrifying I shall put down. (Is 13:9-11)
>
> "Its [Babylon's] time is near coming, its days will not drag on." (Is 13:22)

Isaiah 40–55 does not use "Yahweh's day" language, unless "day of deliverance" (Is 49:8) riffs on that expression, as does Isaiah 56–66 with the correlative expression "day of redress" (Is 61:2; 63:4). It does emphasize that Yahweh's *ṣĕdāqâ*, Yahweh's act of faithfulness, is near (Is 51:5).

The ultimate day of Yahweh did not arrive within the temporal framework of Isaiah, otherwise we would not be having this discussion. What theological understandings of this fact might emerge from Isaiah?

One understanding is indicated by the transition from Isaiah 1–55 to Isaiah 56–66. These last chapters begin by urging the community to see to the implementing of *mišpāṭ* and *ṣĕdāqâ,* "because my deliverance is near to coming, my *ṣĕdāqâ* [is near] to revealing itself" (Is 56:1-2). As is often the case, it would be an oversimplification to make Yahweh's action conditional on the human action. Yahweh links human *ṣĕdāqâ* and divine *ṣĕdāqâ,* not by making the former a precondition of the latter, but by making the latter a stimulus to the former. Yet there is indeed a relationship between these two, and where there is no human *ṣĕdāqâ,* people cannot expect to see divine *ṣĕdāqâ.* There follows an indictment in Isaiah 57:3-21, with the climax in verses 20-21, which indicates that Judahites are still attached to traditional religion. Yet further divine commitments follow the indictment (Is 57:19), and Yahweh again commissions the raising of a road for or to the people. Yahweh is the high and lofty one, the eternal and Holy One, who revives the spirit of the people who are down and broken—which does not necessarily mean contrite (Is 57:15).

There are certainly passages implying that Yahweh's action can be delayed by human (in)action. Judah has insisted on solving its own problems and finding its own resources and will therefore find that they fail, and further that

> Therefore Yahweh will wait to show grace to you;
> therefore he will arise to show compassion to you.
> Because Yahweh is a God who acts with authority:
> the blessings of all who wait for him! (Is 30:18)

Another possible theological understanding is indicated by the fact that Yahweh implicitly reserves the right to take a broader set of factors into account in deciding when to act, which is part of Yahweh's point to Job in explaining (or declining to explain) why Job's life is not working out in the way he might reasonably have expected. "I, Yahweh, will speed it in its time" (Is 60:22). It has a time of its own within Yahweh's purpose.

Another understanding is suggested by the nonspecific language of some "Yahweh's day" passages, such as Isaiah 13:2-16. While this chapter begins by identifying this prophecy as a pronouncement about Babylon and goes on to identify Yahweh's army as the Medes, the actual Yahweh's day passage lacks specific reference and reads like something more universal, of which the putting down of Babylon by the Medes is one embodiment. So "Yahweh's day" is the day when Yahweh's ultimate purpose is fulfilled, and when Israel and the world make a transition to a new age and a different kind of life and experience in which Yahweh's purpose for the world is implemented rather than frustrated. But that purpose also finds periodic fulfillment within this age as Yahweh acts to implement it in some measure in an event such as the fall of Samaria, the fall of Jerusalem, the fall of Babylon or the restoration of Judah after the exile. When prophets speak of that day as imminent, often they do not distinguish between ultimate fulfillment and interim fulfillment; it is only the event itself and its aftermath that will indicate which it is.

There are many passages where reference to "that day" points away from a time that is imminent and more explicitly suggests the ultimate. Ameliorating warnings about terrible catastrophe, Isaiah 4:2 declares that "on that day Yahweh's branch will be the glory and the splendor, the land's fruit will be the majesty and the beauty, of the people who escaped in Israel." To put it another way, "on that day" there will be a delightful vine to sing about (Is 27:2-6), one that contrasts point by point with the one in Isaiah 5:1-7, one that Yahweh keeps watch over, waters, never gets angry with and fights for rather than against, one that flourishes and fills the world with its fruit. On the other side of the felling of the Davidic tree and the arising of a new shoot from it (and therefore not in the immediate future from the perspective of Isaiah ben Amoz), "on that day Jesse's root that is standing as a standard to peoples—nations will have recourse to him, and his abode will be glorious" (Is 11:10). On the other side of the exile that has not happened in the time of Isaiah ben Amoz, there will be a second exodus: "on that day my Lord will again a second time with his hand acquire the remains of his people that remain," from the different parts of the Middle Eastern and Mediterranean world (Is 11:11). And "on that day you will say, 'I will confess Yahweh: "You were angry with me; your anger turns, and you have comforted me."' . . . On that day you will say, 'Confess Yahweh, call out in his name, cause his deeds to be acknowledged among the peoples, proclaim that his name stands high'" (Is 12:1, 4).

Other similar visions of transformation do not incorporate reference to

"Yahweh's day." Pasturage and farmland will be transformed, and the faithful exercise of authority will characterize them, issuing in peace and the quiet, trusting confidence and rest that Isaiah has urged, when the city is laid low (Is 32:15-20). Pasturage and desert will blossom gloriously, dry land will become wetland, and people will see Yahweh's glory there; blind will see, deaf will hear, disabled will run, mute will shout; exiles will have a dedicated, safe road to get back to Zion with joy (Is 35:1-10). There is thus a contrast between these visions and ones that follow in Isaiah 40–55 that use similar imagery but relate the vision to a particular "day."

Further, Yahweh's ultimate day affects more than merely earthly peoples.

On that day Yahweh will attend
to the army on high, in the heights,
and to the kings of the ground, on the ground.
They will be gathered, a gathering,
captives in a cistern.
They will be imprisoned in a prison,
and after many days they will be attended to.
The moon will know shame, the sun will know disgrace,
when Yahweh Armies has begun to reign
On Mount Zion and in Jerusalem,
and before his elders will be splendor. (Is 24:21-23)

On that day Yahweh will attend,
with his tough sword, great and powerful,
To Leviathan the gliding snake,
to Leviathan the twisting snake;
he will slay the dragon that is in the sea. (Is 27:1)

Such talk of "that day" commonly implies a time that looks suspiciously far away rather than around the corner. The people of God therefore "wait" and "long," they "yearn in the night" and then get up early for the morning worship time to pray (*šāḥar*) that Yahweh will implement all that these visions portray (Is 26:8-9).

The book called Isaiah is wide ranging in the contexts to which it relates and in the complex issues it handles. It knows that nothing is simple, and a significant aspect of its richness is thus that it encourages readers to think through the complexity of key theological questions in a way that will do justice to them and inspire a theology that can be lived with.

SUBJECT INDEX

SCRIPTURE INDEX

Finding the Textbook You Need